Hold'em Wisdom
for all Players

Hold'em Wisdom
for all Players

by Daniel Negreanu

CARDOZA PUBLISHING

Cardoza Publishing is the foremost gaming publisher in the world, with a library of over 200 up-to-date and easy-to-read books and strategies. These authoritative works are written by the top experts in their fields and with more than 9,000,000 books in print, represent the best-selling and most popular gaming books anywhere.

FIRST EDITION
2nd Printing, March 2007

Copyright © 2007 by Daniel Negreanu
- All Rights Reserved -

This material is printed by special arrangement with
Card Shark Media

World Poker Tour cover photo courtesy of WPT Enterprises, Inc.
© 2005 WPT Enterprises, Inc.
- All Rights Reserved -

Library of Congress Catalog Card No: 2006922958
ISBN: 1-58042-210-1

Visit our web site—www.cardozapub.com—or write for a full list of books and computer strategies.

CARDOZA PUBLISHING
P.O. Box 1500, Cooper Station, New York, NY 10276
Phone (800) 577-WINS
email: cardozapub@aol.com
www.cardozapub.com

DANIEL

Kid Poker

Daniel Negreanu, one of the most popular and charismatic players in poker, exudes the confidence of a new generation of poker players raised on video games, the Internet and MTV. Best known for both his aggressive style of play and his amiable personality, Daniel was the leading money-winner in the first few years of the World Poker Tour (WPT). And until the recent dramatic surge in World Series of Poker (WSOP) prize money, he was the all-time money winner in poker tournament history. As of this printing, Daniel's tournament winnings are a staggering $8 million—and growing.

Negreanu's accomplishments include three WSOP bracelets, two WPT championships, Player-of-the-Year awards in both the WPT and WSOP, more than 40 wins in tournaments worldwide, and international stardom as one of the best tournament players in the world.

Negreanu is an esteemed contributor to Doyle Brunson's *Super System 2*, the author of a nationally syndicated newspaper column entitled "Playing Poker with Daniel Negreanu," and a consultant to fullcontactpoker.com, a site he launched in 2003. He appears regularly on TV playing poker against the best players in the world.

Acknowledgments

Poker has been very, very good to me, and I feel compelled to thank those that share the same spirit for the game that I have.

First and foremost, I'd like to thank Steve Miller of Card Shark Media for encouraging me to write these pieces and for helping me reach millions of readers across the USA and Canada. Also, thanks to Avery Cardoza of Cardoza Publishing for making this book happen, and to Tom Mills for his great editing.

From a more personal standpoint, I definitely want to thank my mother, Annie Negreanu, for being the best mother a son could ask for. Also, I thank my father, Constantin, who passed in 1996. I only wish he was around today to see what poker has become and to see that his boy did alright.

To Jennifer Harman, not only the best female poker player in the world, but also a truly great friend, I say thank you. Jennifer has taught me so much about poker, most importantly how to be a professional poker player.

Also, thanks to the "Rat Pack," consisting of Phil Ivey,

John Juanda and Allen Cunningham for sharing so much of their knowledge with me and helping me become the player I am today.

I'm also thankful to all the wonderful friends I've made over the years playing on the poker circuit. The poker community is such a close-knit group and I feel fortunate to be a part of it.

I hope you enjoy reading the book as much as I've enjoyed writing it.

Daniel

Dedicated to the best parents a kid could ask for,
Ana and Constantin Negreanu.

CONTENTS

I.

Introduction

You're holding a book that can really enhance your poker game. I've compiled fifty of my favorite strategy nuggets and thoughts written specifically about today's most popular poker game, Texas hold'em.

Each piece is concise and contains valuable information that will help you at all levels of the game. It's not intended to be a heavy-handed poker encyclopedia, but a fun primer and reference guide that can be read and re-read to help keep important game concepts fresh in your mind.

I'm actually a poker fan first, and a player second. The tremendous growth that poker has seen in recent years—due to fans enjoying the game on television and playing on the Internet—has brought poker into the mainstream. The image of poker as a seedy game, played in dingy environments, is fading fast. Some even call it a sport now—a sport of the mind.

I've really enjoyed writing this book because it's allowed me to give something back to the game that I love so much.

1.

Top Ten Rookie Mistakes

Here is my list of the top ten mistakes rookie players make at the poker table. If you see yourself represented here, it's time to make some changes to your game.

1. Bluffing too much.

Most rookies have watched too many Hollywood movies and have convinced themselves that poker is all about bluffing. Somehow, they think that if they just keep betting, everyone will get out of their way. That's unlikely, because a habitual bluffer is easily identified by his opponents early on.

2. Lack of patience.

Playing poker means you'll go through long stretches of sheer boredom waiting for good cards. Rookies often don't have the patience to wait for quality cards, so, out of boredom, they start playing hands they know they shouldn't.

Don't lose your patience, find it.

3. Playing unaffordable limits.

Nothing is more detrimental to your confidence—and your bankroll—than gambling with money you can't afford to lose. You simply can't make smart decisions when you're also worrying about how you're going to pay the rent if the queen of spades doesn't bail you out on the river. It's very important to play within a budget you feel comfortable with. You'll be able to focus on the game rather than the financial implications.

4. Drinking alcohol while playing.

You need to have all of your wits about you in order to make quality decisions at the table. It's no coincidence that casinos offer free alcohol to customers. Booze clouds your judgment and will have you making plays you wouldn't have considered making with a clearer head.

5. Quitting while you're ahead.

Sorry to burst your bubble, but there is no system for figuring out when it's time to pack up and leave. The worst plan that many rookies utilize is the one where they hit and run by quitting after very small wins, but continue to play when they're behind. If anything, that's the exact opposite of what you should be doing.

When you're winning, you have a powerful table presence that you should exploit. When you're losing, that table image is tarnished and can have a negative effect on your confidence.

6. Playing in tough games.

Beginners, some of whom aren't even all that bad at poker, will often place themselves in games against competition they just can't handle. Rather than playing in smaller limit games against opponents of comparable skill, they prefer to go head to head with the big boys. You can guess how that usually turns out.

7. Elevated ego.

No, you're not as good as you think you are. In fact, you have a lot to learn. The day you realize you know too little about poker is the day you actually might start learning a thing or two.

Know-it-alls generally know very little about what it takes to improve their poker game. It's very important to be objective about your skills and where you might need improvement.

8. Playing too many hands.

Rookies play more hands than they should, not understanding the importance of starting with premium hands in premium situations. Pick up a book or two before sitting down to play, and you'll understand why 9-3 is a bad hand to start with, whether it's suited or not!

With all of the information out there today, there is no excuse for lacking fundamental poker knowledge.

9. Playing on tilt.

Just like a pinball machine that gets banged too hard, a beginner will often short circuit when he loses a couple of bad hands in a row. A tilted player loses all faith in his game plan and will chase bad hands like inside straight draws, even though he knows he shouldn't.

And now, drum roll please—the number one mistake rookie poker players make.

10. Playing too many hours.

Your brain just doesn't function well after spending very long stretches sitting at the table. Rather than getting some rest, and coming back fresh the next day, most beginners end up playing too many hours trying to chase their money back. In the process, they end up throwing away even more.

Your mind plays tricks on you after so many hours, and

you'll often convince yourself that you're playing well. Chances are, you're not.

2.

Top 5 Reasons Why You're Losing at Poker

There's a quote I once heard that I thought was genius: "Poker is a lot like sex. Everybody thinks they are great at it, but most people don't really know what they're doing."

Because of that truth, people generally blame their losing streaks on bad luck. Well, while bad luck can certainly play a role, there might just be other pressing factors for your losing.

Here are the top five reasons.

1. Bad luck.

If this is your worst problem, then, ironically, you're in luck! Why? Poker is a game where luck *does* play a part in how well you do, and bad luck could be the reason you're losing.

However, the longer you play poker, *smartly*, the less likely bad luck will continue as a factor that brings you down. Like all poker players, you have to ride out bad luck streaks. Just don't be foolish and create your own bad luck.

Losing a few sessions in a row can easily be chalked up to bad luck, but if you're habitually losing after months and months of play, chances are bad luck is not the key factor.

Here's a suggestion: Chart your results by the hour. See how you're doing after 500 to 1,000 hours of play before throwing in the towel. If you're still showing a loss after that much play, well, you just might have a problem that has nothing to do with luck.

2. Too predictable.

This is especially true if you were once a winning player against the same opponents and are now losing to them on a regular basis. If you have a very straightforward approach to the game, it could be that your opponents are on to you. Solution: Elevate your game by adding some deceptive plays to your arsenal.

For example, if your opponents have caught on to the fact that you simply never bluff, maybe it's time that you come out of your shell and start making some creative moves.

3. Playing in tough games.

You could be the fifth best poker player in the world, but if you're seated at a table with the top four players in the world, well, you're the sucker!

Game selection is as important to your bankroll as how you play the game. Swallow your pride, put your ego in check, and simply ask yourself this tough question: Are the guys that I play with better than me? If the answer is yes, you need to find a new game against lesser-skilled competitors.

4. Lack of fundamentals.

This is a common reason for losing. But there is some good news: Learning poker fundamentals is as easy as picking up a few great books and working on expanding your knowledge base. Hey, it certainly couldn't hurt.

If you don't have a solid foundation for making poker decisions, you'll always be a step behind. Learn how to play the game the right way by focusing on the basics, and when you get those down, add your own style to the mix.

5. Playing on tilt.

The most significant factor in your overall results is how you handle yourself when you get unlucky. Many players blow a gasket, lose their cool, and their bankrolls soon follow.

Taking a bad beat or two is inevitable. The difference between long-term winners and losers is how bad luck affects their play over the course of the session.

You never want to *chase* your money. You also don't want to lose your patience by playing hands you know you shouldn't be playing. If you simply can't handle the stress related to bad beats, then do yourself a favor and quit before things turn ugly.

Remember, there's always tomorrow. Poker isn't going anywhere.

Table Talk

There are two opposing views on the effectiveness of table talk as a poker tactic.

Chatting at the poker table can give you an opportunity to learn about your opponent's hand, but the risk is that you might actually give away too much information about your own.

Well, if you've seen me play poker on TV, you know how I feel. I'm convinced that when used properly, in the right circumstances and against the right opponent, table talk can help you gain enough information about another player's hand that it's worth the risk.

The juggling act that you face is trying not to spill the beans by divulging too much information about your own hand.

Here are my seven rules for successful table talk that you might want to follow:

1. Avoid table talk if you are a beginner.

If you are just learning the game, don't get caught up in psychological warfare with players who are more experienced than you are. Instead, focus on the fundamentals like understanding the strength of your hand and what your opponents have, before tackling the art of table talk.

2. Avoid talking to great players.

If *you* are up against an expert, chances are he'll be able to read through whatever you're saying and figure you out before you get any information about *him*.

3. Do your talking on your own time.

If an opponent is studying you, you'd be better off sitting still and staring at on one spot on the table. Unless you feel like you can manipulate your opponent into doing exactly what you want him to do, stay quiet.

Now, if you are studying your opponent and he is willing to have a conversation, try this: Ask him some inane question like, "What are winters like in Phoenix?" The way he answers may give you just the clue you need to figure him out.

4. Mix it up.

Okay, I know that lying is sinful, but all is forgiven at the poker table. If people start to peg you as a player who always tells the truth, or always lies about your hand, then all your chatter will do is guide your opponent in the right direction.

If you want to be a table-talker, you'll need to learn to lie with the same tone, mannerisms, and speed as you would if you were comfortably telling the truth. If that's not something you are able to do, then I suggest you keep your mouth shut.

5. Avoid patterns.

I cannot tell you how many chatterboxes I know that clam up like scaredy cats when they are bluffing. They continue to yap away when they have the *nuts*, but when they are in jeopardy they suddenly come down with a case of laryngitis.

Don't be that player. If you can't hold a normal conversation when you're bluffing, don't table talk. You'll risk giving your opponents way too much information about your hand.

6. Have fun and relax.

If you're relaxed when you're talking to your opponent, you increase the chances of him being the same. And when he's relaxed, chances are he'll be less conscious of what information he is giving away.

Let him just go through the motions unaware, enjoying your witty conversation, while you drain information from his reactions. It's cruel, I know, but so effective.

7. Manipulate the weak.

That doesn't sound very nice, but hey, we're talking poker here! The weak players are the ones that you should generally look to exploit with table talk.

Say, for example, you have the nuts and want your opponent to call but notice that he is about to throw his hand away. Say or do something, *anything*, to make him reconsider. Before he lets go of his cards, try something like, "Phew! For a second there it looked like you were going to call me."

Whatever works, right?

There's one last thing to keep in mind. At all times, avoid being rude, vulgar or mean in any way. It's simply unnecessary behavior.

Contrary to popular belief, being a jerk at the poker table does not help your bottom line. People are generally a lot looser with their money when they're having fun. Make people mad, and all that will do is make them harder to beat.

Bottom line: Tell jokes, not insults.

4.

Three Levels of Poker

There are three basic levels of thought when it comes to approaching a poker hand. As your understanding of poker evolves, and your skills improve, you'll reach Levels Four, Five, Six, and so on, but each stage, after the first three, basically repeats.

1. The first thing you need to focus on is, "What do I have?"

That's about as simple as it gets, and that's why it's called Level One.

As a beginning player, you need to be able to look at your cards, look at the board cards, and then figure out what you have and what cards you need. Then, you must factor in the probability of one of your needed cards actually coming.

2. The second thing you need to think about is, "What do my opponents have?"

That's pretty basic as well, and called Level Two.

Once you've figured out what you have, and whether or not it's a good hand, Level Two requires you to consider what your opponents may or may not be holding.

You accomplish this by focusing on their betting patterns, both past and present. Any information you have on your rivals' previous betting history will help you with the current situation. Other things to ponder, even before you get to their betting patterns, include the following: what cards they like to play, how they usually play them, do the opponents like to limp-in or raise with a pair of aces, do they play loosely from early position or are they conservative?

The questions become even more complicated after the flop. Ask yourself, would one opponent bet so much if he had a flush draw? Does another player like to set traps on the flop and then go for the check-raise?

There are so many variables to consider when putting your challenger on a hand, and the best way to figure things out is to ask yourself various questions. Then go to your memory bank for the answers.

3. The third basic principle to think about is, "What do they think I have?"

This is Level Three poker and relates to your table image, meaning how other players perceive you and the way you play your hands.

Remember, while you are busy trying to figure out what your opponents have, they in turn are trying to figure out what you have as well.

For example, if they've been paying attention and saw you bluff several hands in a row, they may have you pegged, making bluffing in this situation less effective for you.

Conversely, they may figure you to be a weak, straight-forward player who never bluffs. In this case, a well-timed bluff may work very well. Since you know they've been studying you too, try to take advantage of your perceived table image whenever you can.

Understanding your table image is important, but feeding your memory bank, by paying attention to the game at all times, is essential. Remembering similar past hand situations, both how you and your competitor played, is crucial to your success in the current hand.

Let's say the last time you flopped top pair you went for the check-raise, and in another hand you flopped a drawing hand and bet right out. Now, if you've flopped top pair again what you need to think about is this: If you bet right out this time, will he put you on a flush draw again, or will he think you're using reverse psychology?

Chances are, if he's perceptive, your opponent will think your bet means you have a draw. What he doesn't know is that you've delved into your memory bank and are using that stored information against him.

As you can probably imagine from this last example, there is no end to the old game of "I know, that you know, that I know, that you know." In essence, this is your introduction to Level Four poker: "What does he think I think he has?"

The levels never really stop and that's when poker becomes more of a chess match. When both you and your opponent know so much about each other that you are constantly mixing up your game, using reverse psychology and maybe even some reverse-reverse psychology, you've reached a whole new plane.

Just remember to always try and stay one step ahead of your opponents and you'll do just fine.

5.

What Are You Looking At?

You've no doubt heard the myth about needing a poker face to play the game well. I'm going to let you in on a little secret today. Poker isn't about reading facial tics—it's about reading people.

What's the difference you ask?

Well, when you hear the term, 'reading your opponent,' it doesn't necessarily mean that you are looking for body language clues. More often than not, the *tells* you're looking for come from reading your opponents' betting patterns.

There is a famous poker player out there who claims that he can "see through your soul." No, he can't. Trust me. Some top pros might want you to believe that type of hype so they can garner a psychological edge over you.

The truth is, an elite poker player doesn't focus much on body language. Instead, he tries to understand how you think based on the hands you play and how you play them. He isn't looking for some obscure nostril flare or eye twitch to make a decision, but you can bet he's delving into his memory bank and comparing notes from previous hands.

He's likely asking himself questions such as, "How much did my opponent bet the last time he was bluffing?" Or, "When he flops three of a kind, does he usually check to trap me or does he bet right out to protect his hand?"

So, those physical tells that television commentators like to go on about are for the most part a bunch of hogwash! Watch me on television and you'll see that I make all kinds of strange faces. Good luck trying to figure out what they mean.

Reading tells and reading people are two separate skills that are often lumped together, but they are, in fact, very different.

Reading *tells* is the ability to recognize the way people look when they are bluffing versus telling the truth. Reading *people* deals more with the ability to understand how someone thinks based on various clues you can put together.

How to Read Tells

The first thing you'll need to do is simply pay attention. This applies not only when you are in a hand, but also when you've folded and are waiting for the next deal. Study your opponents and look for any behavioral patterns you can find.

For example, maybe you see one of your opponents cover his mouth before he pushes in a big bet. After the hand, he shows that he was bluffing. Does he also cover his mouth when he has a strong hand? If not, you may have just picked up a valuable tell.

The more you practice this skill of picking up subtle clues about your opponents, the more pots you'll be picking up.

How to Read People

Now this is really where it's at.

Poker is a game of people, first and foremost, and understanding how an opponent thinks will go a long way toward giving you a significant advantage over him.

To do this, you need to think like a detective by putting clues together and trying to understand what they mean. This could be anything from studying what your opponent is wearing to ascertaining what he does for a living. People unwittingly reveal all kinds of clues about themselves.

Here's a case study:

A man with a hairy chest wearing an unbuttoned open shirt that reveals tons of gold chains sits at your table. He smells a little bit off, stacks his chips recklessly and smokes incessantly. His fingernails are dirty and he won't stop shaking his knee.

Right off the bat, you know a good amount about this person, because you've already asked yourself this important question: Is he likely to be patient, scared, and conservative, or is he more likely to be an impatient, fearless, and aggressive player?

If you guessed the former, you may want to find a new hobby like checkers or something.

For more clues, now go ahead and ask him some questions. "What do you do for a living?" is always a good one.

If he says he's a lawyer, well, you know who not to trust, right?

If he claims he's a math teacher, chances are you're dealing with a very analytical player.

Or, if he swears he's a Sunday school teacher, you might be dealing with someone who is uncomfortable telling lies, or, in this case, already bluffing.

The bottom line: Reading tells and reading people are both very real skills, and, when used together, make for a deadly combination.

6.

Home Run Hitters vs. Small Ball Players

Anyone who knows anything about my approach to no-limit hold'em understands that I'm a firm believer in the *small ball* theory rather than the riskier *all-in* approach to the game.

Small ball, as it relates to poker, is a grind-it-out style of play that, while still aggressive, doesn't rely on big home run heroics. The small ball tournament approach looks to steadily increase your chip count, while trying to avoid big risks in marginal situations.

Before continuing, I must add the following disclaimer: Small ball is an extremely advanced strategy and should only be used by players with a good amount of experience.

The reason that's true is because small ball depends heavily on hand reading skills. On top of that, it entails playing a lot of hands, and being faced with decisions that are more difficult.

Phil Ivey, Phil Hellmuth, Michael "The Grinder" Mizrachi, Erick Lindgren, Gus Hansen, myself, and a slew of other top no-limit hold'em players, all use the small ball approach. It's hardly a coincidence.

Strangely enough, the advice I give the novice with regard

to small ball is precisely the opposite advice I give to the advanced player.

Beginners should stick to the home run approach by playing big bet poker with all-in bets when necessary. While that's not the optimal long-term strategy, it will help neutralize a better player's advantage over them.

Think about that for a minute.

When a rookie keeps going all-in every hand, he takes all the play away from his more experienced competition. The small ball expert wants to see a lot of flops cheaply so he can outplay novices after the flop. The all-in strategy negates that advantage, and the pro is relegated to being just another player waiting for a good hand.

Now, of course, I'm not suggesting that you go all-in crazy. Large raises can often accomplish the same objective.

As a rule, a beginning player should instead look to make large raises before the flop. When the blinds are $400-$800 with a $100 ante, the home run hitter should be raising to $4,000. There is really no good reason to change the raise amount based on your cards. In fact, by raising the same amount with pocket aces as you would with A-10, you give away less information to your opponents.

Conversely, a small ball veteran would likely raise the pot to about three times the big blind. So, if there are nine people seated at the table, with $2,100 in blinds and antes, the expert would raise about $2,000 to $2,400.

While the beginning player was risking $4,000 to win $2,100 (laying nearly 2 to 1 odds on the hand), the small ball player is getting much better value—about even money.

Another thing to think about is that the home run hitter won't get as much action as will the small ball player. Against the slugger, the big blind would have to call an additional $3,200 to see the flop; against the small ball player, he might only have to call $1,200, getting almost 3 to 1 odds.

This is the essential difference that makes the home run style much easier to play. Sluggers simply don't have to make as many decisions after the flop. Small ball players, however, desperately want to see a lot of flops so that they can force opponents into more difficult decisions.

The very best small ball players make poker look like controlled chaos. They're seemingly involved in every hand and are always keeping opponents on their heels.

Consider one more sports analogy—boxing. The small ball player continually throws jabs while always keeping his guard up. His goal is to wait for the opportunity when his opponent makes a big mistake and opens up his chin.

That's when he socks it to him with the big uppercut!

7.

To Show or Not to Show? That is the Question

There are two schools of thought when it comes to revealing your cards after everyone else has folded and the hand is over. One asks, why would you? Why give your opponents free information about how you play when they didn't pay for it?

While I totally understand and respect this strategy, I believe that in certain situations, it can be advantageous to show opponents your cards. When you watch me play poker on television, notice that I often show my hand. Of course, I'm not doing this randomly. My reasoning is calculated, and designed to give me an edge that I can exploit later in the game.

Think of it like this: I'm planting seeds that I can harvest later. You might consider doing a little poker gardening yourself.

Here's how showing your hands can work to your benefit, particularly when you're up against novice players.

1. Showing a bluff.

Revealing your bluff hand might be good for your table

image after you've successfully pushed your opponents out of the hand.

Bad players tend to have very long memories. By showing just one of your bluffs, they may conclude that you try to steal *all* of the pots, *all* of the time. Later in the game, when you are dealt the best hand, you'll benefit because they will call you more often than they should.

2. Showing a strong hand.

There are two ways to make the most of this situation. If you are up against a weak player, showing him that you bet a strong hand will often allow you to bully him for the rest of the night. It will put the notion in his mind that when you bet, it's always because you have great cards, even if you don't.

The other benefit in revealing a strong hand is that it may help to keep an aggressive player off your back. Aggressive players are the toughest to face, and quite frankly, you don't want them attacking you.

An aggressive player will be less inclined to attack if he has evidence that you weren't messing around when you raised him earlier. Befriending an aggressive player by revealing your hand can actually tame him.

You know what they say: Keep your friends close and your enemies closer.

3. Setting up a play.

Revealing a hand can have its benefits anytime you make a play that is out of the norm for you. Let's say, for example, in a limit hold'em game, you usually raise the bet when holding top pair. Only this time, you just call your opponent on the flop and then raise him on the turn when a safe card hits.

If your opponent folds, showing your hand may lead him to believe that you make this play often. In the future, when you just call on the flop, he may worry that you'll raise him on the turn.

Conversely, if you raise on the flop, he may think it's more likely you have a drawing hand, since your track record suggests that you always raise on the turn with top pair.

Here's a very important rule. Don't engage in this type of psychological warfare if you are a novice player. In fact, you'd be much better off never revealing your hand unless you are obligated to do so.

And one last piece of advice: Don't show your cards when squaring off against great players. Revealing your hand is much more effective against more easily manipulated opponents.

Showing or not showing cards will always be a topic of great debate amongst poker's elite. In my book, revealing your hand to a weak opponent can often be an effective and profitable tactic.

8.

Beating Up on the Weak Player

If someone describes your playing style as weak, you're in lots of trouble. You'd better make changes to your game quickly to shed that reputation.

If you want to win at the poker table, focus on the weak players. Rather than duke it out with strong, aggressive players, you'll risk less and win more in the long run, playing against timid, passive players.

In order to pound on the shaky players properly, the first thing you'll need to do is identify them. There are generally a few clues that you can look for, that, while not always accurate, could be signs nonetheless.

1. How he dresses.

A player who dresses conservatively will generally play poker that way. If he dresses loudly, he'll more than likely play aggressively or flamboyantly.

2. How he talks.

This is in line with the previous clue. If a player is quiet or timid in the way he speaks, chances are that's how he'll play poker. Conversely, if you're dealing with a boisterous or overexcited talker, he'll probably be an aggressive player.

3. Does he raise before the flop or just call?

If he likes to limp in on a regular basis, you might be dealing with a weak player.

4. Does he like to bet, or check and call?

An aggressive player is a bettor, while a weaker player tends to check or just call others' bets.

Once you've identified the weak players at your table, it's time to strategize against them. Playing against a weak player is, without a doubt, the easiest type of opponent to face. In fact, your cards often don't even matter since your inferior foe plays so predictably.

The key principle to think about is to basically pound him like an anvil! Do it repeatedly—like the school bully who steals his target's lunch money—until he starts to stick up for himself. If he keeps giving it up, you keep taking it.

Hey, no one said poker was supposed to be fair.

When you have position on an ineffective player it makes it that much easier. What you really want to look for are opportunities to get the weak opponent heads-up.

How do you do that? Well, when the helpless one limps into a pot you try to isolate him with a decent-sized raise. That will often knock everyone out but the timid player. Now you've got him where you want him. If the player is extremely weak, it doesn't even matter if you have a 7-2 in your hand.

You really aren't playing your hand anyway, you're playing the player.

If you are able to get the weak player heads up, with position, you'll let his actions, or lack of them, dictate what you should do. If he bets the flop, you can be pretty sure he has a good hand. If you don't flop a very good hand, now would be an excellent time to fold. You might be playing the player, but you can't ignore his bet entirely.

If he checks the flop, then you should bet, regardless of what you have. If, however, your inept opponent check-raises you, run and hide! Unless, of course, you flop a strong hand yourself. The only time you may want to check is if you flop the nuts and want to give him a free card. Otherwise, you should always bet the flop and look to win the pot right there.

The tricky decision comes when the weak player decides to just call, which he will often do. At that point you have to make a game-time decision as to whether your opponent flopped a drawing hand or a made hand.

Since your opponent is weak, he won't give you much information about his hand by the way he plays it. Generally, an inadequate player will check and call with either a made hand (like top pair) or a flush draw.

As a rule, proceed cautiously if a weak player calls you on the flop. If you have a good hand, by all means, bet. But if you are bluffing, lean towards checking on the turn card since the weak player has shown some interest.

There is an old adage in poker that I think sums up that last point: "If you bluff a bad player you then become one." Stay aggressive against weak players, but don't get caught running without the ball when they show interest in the flop.

9.

Bullying a Bully

It can be really frustrating to have an extremely aggressive player at your table that just won't seem to leave you alone. No matter what you do, the bully keeps coming after you, especially if you aren't getting any good cards of your own.

Hopefully, after reading this, you'll have all the tools you need to fight the good fight and start pounding back. If you know anything about a bully, you know that if you stand up to him, he'll usually run away and hide.

Let him run, but get his chips first.

To accomplish that, the first thing you need to understand is the bully's biggest weakness. It's that he likes to play lots of hands, and, when he does, he'll play them aggressively. Sooner or later, he'll cross the line between good, solid, aggressive play and become a maniac who bluffs too much and plays wildly.

What you need to do is exploit his aggressive tendencies so that they work in your favor.

When you sense that a bully is crossing that line, take a deep breath and give him as much rope as he needs to hang himself. By that I mean, trap him with your good hands and let him bluff off his money to you. There is actually a poker term for this maneuver: **collecting bullets**.

Collecting bullets is an excellent way to keep a poker tyrant off your back. Try slowplaying to trap your opponent. This passive and clever tactic will win pots from the bully that, had you otherwise bet, would likely have prompted him to fold his cards.

Remember, a bully looks to pounce on perceived weakness, just like one of those hooligans did in grade school. On the playground, you'd eventually need to stand up to the tormentor to get him off your back. In poker, though, you want to let him feel like he can run over you all day. Indeed, when you have a monster hand, your greatest desire is that he will pounce all over you. Let him do all the betting for you.

Or, as a friend of mine, and fellow professional player, Layne Flack, says, "Why do the pushin' when the donkey will do the pullin'."

It's very important and also financially rewarding to recognize situations where slowplay checking will win you more money than betting. The bully who bets when you check, but folds when you bet, is the perfect target for bullet collecting.

Now, I don't want to leave you with only one anti-bullying strategy or you could end up like a sheep to the slaughter. There is more to it. There are times when you don't want to appear to be a pushover by letting the bully run the show. The advice I've given thus far works best when your opponent has position on you throughout the hand.

However, when you have position on him, then it's time to stand up and show him who's boss.

When you're in position, meaning that you are seated to the bully's left, be a thorn in his side by raising and reraising to take control of the hand. He usually won't have a strong enough hand to play and will fold.

Here's the most crucial concept to master: Always make

the bully think twice about stealing the blinds. You must make him believe that he could run into a buzzsaw at any moment—that buzzsaw being you! Once you've tamed the aggressive opponent, the door for you to become the bully has just opened.

Since you're now the bully, your opponents will be leery of you and won't want to mess with you too often. Take advantage of this situation by stealing their blinds. If the other players don't stand up to you, keep being the aggressor and punish them until they do.

And one last thought. Once you become the bully, beware of those motivated players who will try to take you down. Being bullied or being the bully both come with danger.

10.

The Five Times Rule

I'm assuming that many of you reading this book would consider yourself a beginning or novice poker player. If so, then the following no-limit Texas hold'em advice might just be perfect for you.

There are a variety of poker books available that discuss what hands you should be starting with in tournament poker, but there isn't enough advice about how and how much you should be betting on those hands.

Well, I'd like to introduce the *five-times-the-big-blind-rule* to you. It's basically as simple as it sounds.

You should be raising five times whatever the big blind is. If the blinds are $25/$50, and you are the first one to enter the pot, you should raise the bet to $250 if you decide to play the hand. What this maneuver will do is give you a chance to really protect your hand by making your opponents pay a heavy price to see the flop.

Strangely enough, it's the exact opposite advice I'd give to an advanced player.

For the advanced player, I'd recommend raising to just two

and a half to three times the big blind. Why? It's simple. A more skilled player makes better decisions after the flop than does a novice. So, as a beginning player, you want to see fewer flops for that very reason.

Try not to let a more experienced player get to the flop because his skill advantage will then come into play. Your edge, as a rookie, will come from starting with stronger hands and betting them more aggressively before the flop.

Now what if someone else has called the big blind in front of you? Well, the fives times rule now becomes the *seven-times-rule*. If a player limps in for $50, you'd want to make it even more expensive to see the flop by making it $350. This betting system isn't without it's holes, mind you, but it will help less experienced players avoid getting involved in too many complex decisions after the flop.

Always remember the general theory: If a hand isn't good enough to raise with, then you should fold it.

Raise or fold poker is the best approach for a new player. On that note, what should you do if someone has raised the pot in front of you?

If the blinds are now, for example, $50-$100, and another player comes in for a raise of $300, you should still use the five times rule. Only this time, you'll be raising it to five times the last bet. Five times the last bet of $300 is $1,500, and that's the bet I'd advise you to make.

This strategy might seem a little too aggressive, but I assure you, it will give a beginning player the best opportunity to succeed. As your game improves, and you feel more comfortable making good decisions after the flop, then you can make smaller raises before the flop and start entering the pot for about three times the blind.

There is one last rule I'd like to share with you that deals with pre-flop betting in tournament poker. It's called the **30 percent rule**.

If your standard raise of five times the big blind is more than 30 percent of your total stack, then just go ahead and move all in.

This is one of the deadliest weapons in your arsenal, as it's extremely difficult to defend against. In order for your opponents to call such a large bet, they'll have to have a premium hand like A-A, K-K, or A-K. They can't outplay you anymore since your decision has already been made.

It's important to remember that following these rules isn't necessarily the optimal strategy, but they will help any beginner go farther in tournaments and give him or her a much better chance of actually cashing in. It's certainly not how I, as a professional player, choose to play, but it is a style that gives me fits to play against.

It forces a pro to rely more heavily on the luck of the cards, and as a novice, that's exactly what you want to do.

11.

Aggressive Play vs. Conservative Play

I'd like to set the record straight right here and now; if you want to win big money playing tournament poker you are going to have to play aggressively. It's simply not a coincidence that all of the players you see on TV winning millions of dollars have one thing in common: aggressiveness.

So what exactly does it mean to be aggressive at the poker table? Well, the idea behind it is to push the limits, fight for lots of pots, and get active in the game.

The opposing strategy would be to sit back, wait for premium hands, and hope that someone plays with you when you do. There are several key problems with the conservative strategy.

1. You won't be dealt enough premium hands to stay afloat.

In no-limit hold'em tournaments, the blinds and antes continue to escalate, which force you to gamble. If you just sit there and wait for A-A or K-K, you'll end up anteing yourself to death!

2. You'll become too predictable.

If everyone sees that you aren't playing very many hands, they'll know when you do enter a pot that you have a monster. Thus, if they have marginal hands, they won't give you the action you desire.

3. No one will fear you.

If your opponents pick up on the fact that you're playing very conservatively, they will repeatedly attack your blinds knowing that you won't call unless you happen to have a strong hand. That's not the image you want. You'd be much better off known as a pest who won't let the others breathe.

The key to being a successfully aggressive player is to do so in a selective manner. Going overboard with a hard-hitting approach can easily turn into just being reckless. In fact, let me introduce a new term: cautious aggression. While those two words would seem to contradict each other, they really don't at all. Here's how a cautiously aggressive player approaches no-limit play.

A cautiously aggressive player will raise more than his fair share of pots. He's looking to pick up the blinds, first, or the pot on the flop, second, while hoping to make a strong hand, third. If he finds any resistance from his opponents, he'll duck and cover by throwing his cards away unless he has a very strong hand himself.

If you think of it in boxing terms, a cautiously aggressive player will throw lots of jabs but will always guard his chin. He's constantly jabbing while dodging his foe's punches. When his adversary gets sloppy and leaves his own chin open, the cautiously aggressive player will send him to the canvas with one knockout punch.

On the surface it seems like a brute, chaotic approach, but

realistically, it's all rooted in basic mathematical rules. Let me show you what I mean.

At a nine-handed table, the blinds are $400/$800 with a $100 ante. Already there is $2,100 in the pot ($400 small blind, $800 big blind, and $900 in antes). An aggressive player may decide to raise the bet to $2,000, risking $2,000 to win $2,100 if everyone folds.

One thing we know about hold'em is that it's very difficult to pick up a premium two-card combination. If the aggressive player is up against a table full of conservative opponents, he'll grab the blinds well over 50 percent of the time.

But what about those times when it doesn't work?

If an opponent does call, the aggressive player must now proceed with caution. Moreover, if the conservative opponent reraises, the cautiously aggressive player must make a key adjustment by cutting his losses, throwing away the hand, and trying to steal the next pot.

That is, of course, unless the aggressive player himself has a premium hand. When that occurs, he gets a chance to throw that knockout punch. Since he's been playing so many hands, the aggressive player is more likely to get action even when he has the nuts. So again, it's jab-jab-jab, duck and cover, then throw the knockout punch.

Everybody hates playing against an aggressive player, and for good reason. They are difficult to read and they're always putting the pressure on you. Why not be that guy? Why not be the bully pushing everyone else around? You are there to win after all.

12.

The Deadly All-In Bet

One of the things viewers like most about watching no-limit Texas hold'em on television is the all-or-nothing nature of a game. It's a battle where the player, at any point, can decide to risk it all on the turn of a card.

The all-in bet is certainly exciting, and it's also a very deadly weapon, especially in tournament poker where the blinds escalate rapidly. When used properly, all-in betting can have a neutralizing effect on even the world's greatest players. In fact, if you found yourself in a situation where you were facing professional champions like Johnny Chan or Phil Ivey, the all-in move might just be your only hope.

Here's why it works.

Only strong hands can call.

Once you've made an all-in bet, it forces opponents to have a premium hand in order to call you. When all of your chips are in the pot, opponents can't outplay you anymore because your decision-making process is already complete.

If you're a novice player, the last thing you want to do is

be involved in difficult situations against a superior player after the flop. So consider making your big move before the flop, and turn a world-class cardshark into nothing more than just another player waiting for a premium hand.

While he's waiting, you'll be picking up valuable blinds and antes.

Even when you get caught, you can still win.

The second reason the all-in move is so effective is that even when you get caught with your hand in the cookie jar, you can still win the pot.

Let's say you go all-in on the button with a trash hand like A♥6♦. The big blind picks up a hand like K♠K♣ and calls. Well, you're obviously in trouble, but it's nowhere near as bad as you might think. You'll outdraw the cowboys and win the pot over 28 percent of the time.

Now, if the players in the blinds are top-notch and are waiting for big pairs before they'll play against you, you'll pick up the blinds a very high percentage of the time. And when you add in the success rate of your hand outdrawing a calling opponent, it makes the all-in play effective in most situations.

Math is on your side.

In tournament poker, the game is played with blinds as well as antes. Winning a hand where absolutely nobody calls is often an excellent result and a great way to increase your stack size—risk free.

Let's say, for example, that the blinds are $200/$400, with eight players tossing in an ante of $50 each. There is $1,000 in the pot. Everyone folds to you. You're holding A♠-3♣ on the button and have $10,000 left.

If you go all-in and nobody calls, you'll have increased your stack size by 10 percent simply by having the guts to risk it all.

Even if your opponents call you with a better hand 10 percent of the time, the play would still be profitable in the long run.

Why? As I explained earlier, even a hand like A-6 will beat a pair of kings close to 30 percent of the time.

So, nine times out of ten you'll end up with $11,000 in chips by picking up the blinds and antes. One out of ten times, you'll either be done for the day, or get lucky, and amass $20,400 in chips.

Now, remember, this isn't a foolproof system, and it isn't the optimal strategy for a top professional. However, it is the best way for a beginning player to neutralize a professional's significant skill advantage.

One last thing: If you're contemplating an all-in play, it's also extremely important to factor in your stack size in relation to the blinds. The larger the discrepancy, the less effective the all-in move becomes.

Suppose that in the previous example, you now have $100,000 in chips instead of $10,000. Moving all-in with a trash hand is no longer a good strategy, even for a beginner. Risking $100,000 and your whole tournament life to win a measly $1,000 simply isn't worth it.

13.

Betting Basics: When Less is More

Situations will arise in no-limit Texas hold'em when a smaller bet will actually give you more bang for your buck. More specifically, there are times when betting half the pot will give you the same amount of information as betting the whole pot.

This is a relatively simple concept, especially among top tier players, but it's a strategy that many novice and average players haven't fully grasped.

Let's look at an example to help clarify this point. Suppose you are playing no-limit hold'em and raised before the flop with A-10. Only the player in the big blind called you, so you continue play heads-up with $700 in the pot.

The flop comes K♣8♠4♦. The big blind checks to you. You decide to bet in the hope that your opponent missed the flop and will fold. The question is, how much should you bet?

Well, if you bet the whole pot, $700, you'll definitely find out if your opponent is serious about continuing with the hand. If he calls the pot-sized bet, chances are he has a better hand than your ace high.

While we know we can get that information with a $700 bet, the pertinent questions are: Do you really need to risk the whole $700 to gather that information? Would the outcome be any different had you bet, say, $450?

Probably not. A pot-sized bet and a bet of approximately one-half the pot will yield about the same information. However, the smaller bet is often a much better choice for several reasons:

1. When you are bluffing, you'll be risking fewer chips when you get caught.

Remember, if you are attempting to flat-out steal the pot, betting one-half, three-quarters, or even the full pot will all generally give you sufficient information as to whether your opponent hit the flop.

So in this situation, why risk betting the whole pot when a smaller bet would accomplish the same objective?

2. When you actually have a good hand and want your opponents to play with weaker hands, they'll be more likely to call a bet of one-half the pot rather than a full pot-sized bet.

If you have a *monster* hand and are looking for action, betting half the pot will get you a few more loose calls, and that's exactly what you want.

3. The math is on your side.

Virtually every poker situation can be broken down into a simple mathematical formula. If there is $600 in a pot and you bet $600, you'll be getting even money on your proposition. That means, in the long run, you'd have to win that pot half of the time to make it a profitable play. (Note: There are other factors that come into play on the next two cards, but let's ignore that for this example.)

When you consider that the hand will play out almost identically with a $400 bet, you'll see that, mathematically, it often makes sense to choose the smaller bet.

If you bet $400, you'd be risking $400 to win $600, meaning that you'd be getting 3 to 2 odds rather than even-money. The smaller bet will achieve virtually the same result as the bigger bet but would only have to pay off 40 percent of the time rather than 50 percent of the time had you bet the whole pot.

You will rarely see a top professional bet all of what's in the pot when you watch poker on television. They'll vary their bets generally between one-third, one-half, and three-quarters of the pot. They understand that by keeping the pots smaller, they'll have more control over the outcome. And that's just what they want—to maintain control of the table.

Amateurs, on the other hand, will often make oversized bets out of fear. They worry that a superior player will be able to outplay them if they don't make a sizeable bet. Frankly, that thinking isn't too far off base.

Playing small-bet poker is for professionals and for those who aspire to improve their games to a professional level. If that's not where you are, it just might make sense for you to swing for the fences.

14.

The Value of Suited Cards

In Texas hold'em it would seem pretty obvious that a **suited hand**—both cards being of the same suit—is better than an unsuited, or offsuit hand.

It doesn't take a genius to figure out that K♥J♥ is a better starting hand than K♠J♦, but the real question is, how much better is a suited hand versus an unsuited hand?

To better understand that question, it's important to note a few key factors that distinguish these two hands. The main one being that suited hole cards will only complete a flush about 5 percent of the time.

That certainly doesn't seem like much, but poker is a game of slim edges and subtle nuances. While you'll only make that flush one in twenty times, having four cards to a flush draw can also win you the pot in other ways.

For example, if you were to flop a flush draw you might try a semibluff, or bet *on the come*. This would give you two ways to win: You either complete your flush, or your bet scares everyone else out of the pot and you win it right there.

There are even more ways that suited cards can be of

benefit. Let's say you had that K♥J♥ hand and the flop came 8♥5♥2♦ giving you a flopped flush draw. In this case, you could continue on to the river in the hopes of catching your flush. Sometimes, though, you'll catch a pair of jacks or kings along the way that could also win you the pot.

Now, compare that with the K-J offsuit. This unsuited hand would probably be forced to fold on the flop while the suited hand could take the pot.

One more consideration in favor of the suited hand is that you'll often win very large pots when you do complete a powerful flush. Whether playing limit or no-limit, it's a hand that can pay off big dividends in the right situations.

Based on all this information, it would seem that being suited is a monstrous advantage. There are drawbacks, however, especially for beginning players who fall in love with these drawing hands.

Hey, I don't blame them, suited cards can be tempting to play, but players will too often use the fact that a hand is suited as an excuse to play all sorts of trashy cards.

I don't care if your 7-2 is suited or not, it's still a garbage hand! The same holds true for a 9-3, 10-4 or Q-2. A hand being suited just isn't worth the trouble it can cause.

It can also be very costly to your bankroll if you are always chasing flush draws, especially if you are playing no-limit hold'em. Ponder this one: Having a four card flush draw, after the flop, sure feels like a powerful hand, but even then you'll only complete your draw about one third of the time. For the record, that means you *won't* complete it two out of three times.

Other problems can arise when you make your flush but still lose the pot to a player that makes a higher flush. Let's say you played a K♣3♣ and made a powerful flush on a final board that reads Q♣6♣2♥7♦9♣.

Only one hand could possibly beat you: the ace-high flush.

If, however, you are facing that one hand, it will likely cost you a ton of money since your formerly powerful hand is too strong to surrender. In this case, you'd be destined to lose all your chips when your opponent goes all-in.

So what then is the final word on suited cards?

Well, they're obviously better than unsuited cards, but not as much as you might think. Beginning players often misplay suited hands by gambling on the slim odds that they'll make their flush. Conversely, a real pro knows the true value of these hands and gets the most out of them. For him, suited cards give him even more weapons to win the pot. He knows that suited cards open up options for landing the flush, playing a semibluff, hitting top pair, or folding the hand if the flop comes up dry.

15.

Stealing Blinds

During televised poker tournaments, you'll often here the commentators talk about **stealing blinds**.

They are referring to a situation when a player, holding a junk hand, raises before the flop, hoping to win the blinds and antes without a fight.

It's a very effective and profitable strategy when handled properly. In fact, one of the key elements that differentiate a great tournament player from an average one is the way he utilizes this effective poker tactic.

If you want to be a great player too, you must learn how to perfect this legal form of stealing.

Because blinds and antes escalate so quickly in a tournament, you just don't have all day to wait for premium hands. You have to get involved by trying to steal some blinds just to stay afloat. Otherwise, your stack will dwindle and you'll ante yourself right out of the tournament.

Here are a few important things you need to think about when attempting to steal blinds.

1. Who's in the Big Blind.

When you're considering raising the big blind, it's extremely important to consider who the player is and how he plays. If he's a very loose, aggressive type, then attempting to steal his blind might prove foolish since he will defend it much of the time.

Instead, look to attack the blind of a tight or weak player; you know, the Rock of Gibraltar who only plays when he has aces or kings. He should be your target since you'll get away with this highway robbery often enough to make the play profitable.

2. Your Position at the Table.

Stealing blinds from late position works better than from early position for one simple reason: there are fewer players to act behind you. If you are trying to steal the blinds from first position at a nine-handed table, you'd have to get by eight other players, hoping none of them pick up a hand worthy of a call. That's unlikely. If, however, you attempt to steal from the button position, you'd only have to contend with two players, the little blind and the big blind.

3. Your Table Image.

If you've been pegged as an overly aggressive bluffer, it will become more difficult for you to steal their blinds. If, for example, they've watched you raise three hands in a row, and you also had to show a junk hand like 7-2 offsuit, then your steal attempts will likely be contested, as your cover has been blown.

So, if you feel like your competitors are on to you, it's time to throw them a curve ball and wait for a strong hand to bust them out.

Conversely, if your opponents see you as a rock, you then need to exploit that image by being selectively aggressive. It should be easier for you to steal blinds with a tight image, but you don't want to overdo it, because you'd be risking your image. It's a balancing act that you'll get the hang of with some experience.

4. Your Stack Size.

If you find yourself short-stacked in a tournament, it will have a major effect on your ability to use blind stealing as a weapon. Since other players will realize that you aren't a major threat to their stack, they might decide to play marginal hands against you hoping to knock you out.

So ideally, as a short stack, you want to avoid stealing blinds entirely. But if you feel like you've found a truly good situation to attempt it, put all of your eggs in one basket and go all-in.

If, however, you find yourself sitting pretty with a big stack, use all of that muscle to collect more chips off of the shorter stacks.

There's an old saying, "Making your first million is the hard part. Once you do that, making money is easy."

That's what life is like as a big stack. You have the luxury of being able to mug them in broad daylight against shorter-stacked opponents who know full well that you are stealing their blinds, but simply can't do anything about it.

To become an accomplished blind stealer you need to really pay attention to everything that's going on at the table. It takes more than random thought. You need to focus on these key factors: whose blinds should you steal, what seat you're in, do opponents see you as a thief, and how much ammunition you have.

One last thing, keep an eye out for the player who gets frustrated by your steals. His blind is usually up for grabs!

16.

Be Careful What You Learn on TV

While watching televised poker is an excellent way to learn how to play the game, you really need to be careful about how you interpret what you're seeing.

The key point to remember is that you're watching an edited-down poker show. You're not seeing all the hands played, and that can give you a skewed version of what is really happening.

For example, you might have seen me make a bluff in a certain situation that looked foolish because my opponent called. What you might not have seen, however, is how that *silly* bluff paid off later in the game.

There is always more to the story than what you see on television.

ESPN's coverage is fantastic, but the product is basically a highlight reel of an all-day final table. It would be impossible to tell the whole story in the amount of airtime that they have, so you're left seeing crowd-pleasing confrontations like A-K against a pair of jacks.

You might be wondering how these players get so many

great hands. Well, they don't. You're seeing the most exciting hands from a nine-hour final.

The Travel Channel's poker show, *World Poker Tour*, is a little closer to reality. Two hours are dedicated to each WPT broadcast, and the final table generally lasts between four to five hours. However, there are also inherent problems with learning from this show.

Although you're seeing a much higher percentage of hands, play is distorted by the fact that the blinds escalate so quickly that the element of skill is reduced. As a result, you'll see players going all-in with K-5 and other players calling with hands like K-10.

That's not real poker, and if you operate this way in a normal tournament setting, you're playing far too recklessly and aggressively.

Television's best teaching tool is undoubtedly GSN's *High Stakes Poker*. This program brings together professionals and amateurs, including the likes of Los Angeles Lakers owner Dr. Jerry Buss and Las Vegas casino owner Bob Stupak, in an actual cash game setting. The blinds don't escalate and the goal isn't necessarily to get all the money.

Players compete for cash that they put up themselves. I actually plopped down a million bucks to play in this game. Sure, I was paid $1,250 per hour to be on the show, but if the cards didn't go my way, I could have lost my entire investment.

High Stakes Poker takes 24 hours of footage and breaks it down into a 13-week series. The play is very sophisticated and as close to watching high stakes live poker as you're going to get. Even with this show, I'd add the following caution at the bottom of the screen: Viewer discretion is advised. Do not try these plays at home!

Why? Again, the play is very advanced. Copying these moves and trying them on your buddies at your home game might not work so well. Yes, some of these plays can be deadly in the right hands, but they can also ruin an inexperienced player who attempts them.

Still, watching poker on television is the best way to learn how to play no-limit hold'em—short of actually sitting down at a real table. The key is to understand what you're watching and take everything with a grain of salt.

It's important to understand that players on ESPN don't get better cards than those on The Travel Channel. On top of that, television likes to show the craziest hands. Going all-in with J-6 isn't such a great idea, even if you've seen Gus Hansen try it on the World Poker Tour.

By all means, learn what you can from the professionals on television, but understand you're seeing only the tip of the proverbial poker iceberg.

17.

Pondering Pocket Jacks

Many Texas hold'em players hate getting dealt two jacks because they feel they're unlucky with them. Well, chances are, it isn't that they're unlucky with these cards. They're simply overvaluing the hand and misplaying it.

In hold'em, the best hands you can get are A-A, K-K, Q-Q, and then J-J. However, there is a significant difference between the strength of the jacks and the queens. With queens, there are only two **overcards**—cards higher than a queen— that could hit on the flop and make Q-Q vulnerable.

With pocket jacks, however, there are three overcards that could flop, making the hand more difficult to play. And by the way, this situation happens quite often.

If an overcard doesn't flop, you still have a whole new set of potential worries, such as coordinated boards like: 4-5-7, 3-4-5, 6-7-8. If an opponent is playing a little pair, slowplaying a bigger pair, or is lucky enough to flop a straight, you're doomed.

Pocket jacks is the one hand that seems too strong to fold yet not strong enough to hold if there is much action ahead of you. If you're playing a structured limit hold'em game, the impact isn't as severe. However, in no-limit hold'em where your entire bankroll is in jeopardy, pocket jacks must be played very carefully.

In fact, in a no-limit game, it's not difficult to picture situations where you should fold them before the flop. Think about it for a second.

Let's say an early position player raises the blind, and then a very tight player reraises all-in right behind. As you look down at your pocket jacks, the *fourth* best pair in the deck, you have to ask yourself, what in the world could they have?

Well, they could both have a hand like A-K, in which case you'd be getting good odds on your money. More often than not, though, one of them will be holding a pair bigger than yours.

It's not a stretch to imagine that the first player might have a hand like A-Q, and the all-in raiser is sitting with a pair of kings in the hole. In this case, you'd be a 4 to 1 underdog to win the pot if it's played to the end, and that's not a good thing.

There are countless dilemmas you'll face when holding a pair of jacks, and it's the reason so many people despise the hand.

Frankly, unless a jack hits the flop, you'll never feel too safe. Now, that's not to say that you should automatically fold on the flop if you don't catch a third jack, not at all. Instead, try to protect your hand on the flop with a good size bet. But if someone does call, you had better be willing to abort mission. Fast.

For example, if you bet and the flop comes A-9-4, make one stab at the flop, trying to gauge information about your opponent's hand. If he calls or raises in this spot, what do you think he might have? Chances are he's holding an ace, which only gives you a 7 percent chance of winning the pot.

However, if the flop comes 9-6-2, it's tough to fold your

pocket jacks. The only playable hands that can beat you are 2-2, 6-6, 9-9, Q-Q, K-K, or A-A. In this scenario, bet your hand aggressively, but if your opponent raises, wow, now you have a much tougher decision!

The key here, as with most poker problems, is sizing up your opponent. If he holds aces, kings, or queens, would he have raised big before the flop? Is he the type of player that calls with small pairs before the flop? When he flops three of a kind, does he usually bet it aggressively or play it slow to suck more people in?

In the end, you'll have to make a judgment call. Playing pocket jacks makes for some of the toughest decisions you'll ever face in poker, but hey, no one ever said this game would be easy.

18.

What's the Big Deal About Big Slick?

When you watch poker on TV you'll hear the commentators refer to A-K as a monster hand. Commonly known as Big Slick, A-K is often grouped with hands like A-A, K-K, and Q-Q.

This is a big mistake.

Sure, it's nice to look down at your hole cards and find an A-K, but more often than not, if you end up playing a big pot with this hand you'll be statistically behind. The most likely event is a coin flip situation, where the outcome is close to 50-50.

The following statistic should open your eyes a bit. Did you know that a pocket pair of deuces will beat A-K 53 percent of the time?

Yes, that's right. Even a lowly pair of deuces is a favorite over *powerful* Big Slick. It's even worse off against some other premium starting hands it will often face.

Here is how A-K does against the top five pairs:

- Against pocket tens, jacks, or queens, Big Slick will win only 43 percent of the time.

- Versus pocket kings, Big Slick will win only 30 percent of the time.

- And against pocket aces, your A-K in the hole will lose a whopping 93 percent of the time!

As you can see, it's hardly a coin flip when Big Slick is up against these premium pairs, especially against two cowboys or pocket aces. Of course, your opponent won't always have a pair, and when he doesn't, that's when Big Slick starts looking like a monster, especially if there's an ace or a king in your opponent's hand.

If your opponent held K-Q or A-Q unsuited, for example, you would have him dominated, as he would only have one live card (queen) to outdraw you. In either of these scenarios your Big Slick would be a substantial favorite and will win 74 percent of the time.

There is one other interesting group of hands that Big Slick might match up against: two live cards that are suited, like 7♦8♦. In this case, Big Slick will win 58 percent of the time. You're still a real favorite here, and there always seems to be someone who'll be willing to play you.

These examples give you a little statistical background on this enigma of a hand. In some cases Big Slick is quite strong, while in others it's extremely vulnerable.

In knowing this, the key to playing A-K before the flop is to avoid getting involved in big pots when your entire stake is on the line. Too often when your opponent is willing to put all of his money up against you, he'll have the dreaded

A-A or K-K which would make you a substantial underdog to win the hand.

If you find yourself in a no-limit hold'em tournament looking down at Big Slick, you want to be aggressive with it and attack the blinds. If, however, you receive any resistance from your opponents, you should seriously consider folding the hand and waiting for a better situation.

Here are a few other things to think about before you make a move with Big Slick:

1. How many chips do you have?

If you're short-stacked and need to win a big pot to get back in the game, then you should be very aggressive with Big Slick and go all in. But if you have a good pile of chips and another player at the table raises you big time, well then, you likely don't need to get involved in this marginal situation.

2. How do your opponents play?

This is a very important consideration when making up your mind about playing Big Slick. If the Rock of Gibraltar, a player who is extremely conservative, reraises you, you can be pretty sure that he has a pair that just might be A-A or K-K. On the flipside, if your opponent is wild and reckless, your Big Slick might match up well against a hand like A-J or even K-10 and you'll be in great shape.

The important thing to understand about Big Slick is that it's a drawing hand. Sure, if it's suited, it makes it the most powerful drawing hand you can be dealt in Texas hold'em. But remember, it's still a drawing hand. In the end, it's often only good enough to win with if you pair your ace or king, or get lucky enough to make a straight or a flush.

Playing Big Slick smartly assures you of advancement, and once in awhile it actually earns that monster title so many have given it.

19.

Top Ten Trouble Hands

When you're playing no-limit Texas hold'em, there are certain cards dealt that are known as *trouble hands*. They earn this label because they're difficult to play and oftentimes are dominated by better hands.

Here are the top ten trouble hands to watch out for:

J-8

The trouble with this hand comes when the flop is Q-10-9, giving you the second best straight. If an opponent is playing K-J, a hand most players would play, you're simply doomed to lose everything you have. It would take a miracle, or a ridiculously good read on your part, to get away from this trap.

A-10

While it's an excellent hand in blackjack, the A-10 doesn't fare nearly so well in Texas hold'em. Here's the problem: If you happen to catch another ace on the flop, A-K, A-Q and A-J will all have you beat. Add to that, if the flop comes A-7-4, for example, you'll lose to A-7, A-4, A-A, 7-7, and 4-4. The only time you can really feel safe with A-10 is when you flop two pair or make a straight.

K-Q

It looks like a powerful hand, but you have to be careful with this one. While K-Q will be okay much of the time, if someone has raised the pot in front of you, he may hold A-A, K-K, Q-Q, A-K, or A-Q. Your hand is totally dominated. If the flop is Q-7-2, you'll have a powerful pair with a powerful kicker, but you'll also be trapped. Now you're forced to put more money in the pot and are doomed against Q-Q, K-K, A-A, or A-Q.

A-x suited

These hands look very appealing because they're two parts of a powerful ace-high flush. Be careful, though, not to fall in love with drawing hands in no-limit, as you'll often be forced to pay an all-in bet to try to complete the flush. Another problem with this hand; if you're playing A♥6♥ and flop an ace, your kicker will usually lose to anyone else who is also playing an ace.

K-10

It's just not a very strong hand and should be folded in the face of a raise. If you catch a king on the flop, you have kicker trouble. If you flop the 10, you'll have to worry about A-10 and all of the overpairs: J-J, Q-Q, K-K, and A-A.

A-J

Here's another hand that's ideal for winning small pots but destined to lose big ones unless you make a straight, flush or two pair. If the flop comes, say, A-8-3, and your opponent makes a big bet, you'll be forced to play the guessing game. Does he have A-K or A-Q? Did he flop two pair or maybe three of a kind? Unfortunately, with A-J you'll often be guessing more and winning less.

Q-9

The problem here is the same you faced with the J-8. When a flop comes K-J-10, you'll be doomed to lose all of your money to a player with A-Q. On top of that, if you hit your pair of queens, your kicker will almost surely be beat.

K-J

This is known as the **rookie hand**. It seems too good to fold, but not quite strong enough to raise with. As a general no-limit hold'em rule, if it's not good enough to raise with, then it's not good enough to call with. The big problem with the K-J is that it's dominated by too many hands your opponents would likely play: A-A, K-K, Q-Q, J-J, A-K, and A-J.

J-J

It's the fourth best pocket pair in the deck, but when someone else puts it all-in against you, the decision with pocket jacks is excruciating. Even if you call correctly, and your opponent has a hand like A-K, you'll still only win the pot a little more than half the time. If you guess wrong, and your opponent is holding Q-Q, K-K, or A-A, well, then you're a 4 to 1 underdog.

And the drum roll please...

A-Q

Ask any pro what hand they hate most and A-Q will be right at the top of the list. Why? Well, because it is a strong hand in most situations, but when you're up against the dreaded A-K you'll be almost a 3 to 1 underdog to win the pot!

20.

Isolating Your Opponent in Limit Hold'em

While no-limit Texas hold'em is the game you'll usually see being played for millions of dollars on television, limit hold'em remains the most popular form of poker today.

The games are basically the same; the only difference is how you can bet your hands. No-limit hold'em players understand that their game is one of trapping. However, successful limit hold'em players recognize that their game is all about brute aggression.

I will share with you a very smart play that deals specifically with limit hold'em: isolating your opponent with position.

Position is power in any form of poker, but it's of no use if you don't use that power effectively. How do you do that? Well, here's a good way to start.

Understand, while you'll always want to play powerful position poker, it simply doesn't work in very loose games. It will only prove successful in tighter games where two or three people stay in to see the flop. So, if you're sitting at a table where five or six players continually call to see flops, you'll be better served to tuck this information away until you move up in limits and face more advanced players.

To best explain how to use position as power, let's look at an example.

Let's say you're in a $10/$20 limit hold'em game and everyone has folded to the player directly on your right who raises the bet to $20. You, on the dealer button, look down at a pair of fives and face your first dilemma—call, reraise or fold?

In this case, calling the bet would be the worst of the three choices. A call here would only serve to invite the two players behind you in the blinds to also call. It's important to understand, that while a hand like 5-5 is a favorite heads-up against a hand like A-K, any low pair will fare rather poorly against two opponents.

For that reason, do everything you can to make this a heads-up pot by reraising, or *three-betting* as it's also known, to put extra pressure on the blinds and the initial raiser.

Let's take our example one step further and assume that both players in the blind fold back to the original raiser who calls your raise. Then the flop comes J♠7♣3♦. If your opponent checks on the flop, continue to be aggressive and bet the flop.

Remember, he has no idea what you have.

If your opponent has a hand like A-K or A-Q he might just give up right here fearing that you have a pair of aces or kings. If he calls, well, that's fine, too, because your little pair now becomes close to an 85 percent favorite.

Alternatively, let's suppose the flop comes A-K-9. It certainly doesn't look very good for your little pair of fives. But again, since your opponent has no idea what you have, if he checks, go ahead and bet the flop.

In this case, if your opponent has a hand like 8-8, he'll have a difficult time calling your bet since the flop was lousy for him too. You can win this pot with the worst hand by simply playing your position aggressively.

Here's a key thing to think about: When playing limit hold'em from the power position, keep the lead by making sure that you're the aggressor.

I used a pocket pair of fives in this example, but it really doesn't matter what hand you have when using the isolation play. You can do it with hands like A-K, A-Q, or even 8-9 suited, or K-Q offsuit.

Your goal is to isolate the initial raiser, hope that he misses the flop, and then to apply maximum pressure until he folds.

Of course, you're going to get caught from time to time, but that's okay. The key to using this play effectively is also knowing when to give up on it. If your opponent comes back at with you with a raise, it's time to put on the brakes unless you're confident you have him beat.

21.

Playing Trash Hands

You might ask yourself why a top-notch player like Gus Hansen plays cards like 9-2 offsuit, which you'll see him do in televised tournaments. Any poker book in the world clearly puts a hand like that in the trash category, which means avoid it at all costs.

Hopefully, after you finish reading this book, you'll have a better understanding of the theory behind playing trash hands from time to time, and when it might be right to do so.

The basic principle behind playing a trash hand isn't that you believe your hand has any value at all. It's based on two things:

1. You're representing a strong hand by bluffing.

2. You're hoping your opponents don't have much of a hand.

Let's say, for example, you're playing seven-card stud in an eight-man game and the first four players all fold to you. Your *upcard* is an ace. Unfortunately, for you, your hole cards are absolute trash (7-2).

This isn't a hand you would play under any normal circumstances, but suppose that the three players remaining are all pretty tight. On top of that, their cards don't look threatening; player A shows a 2, player B has a 3, and player C also shows a deuce.

What should you do? Raise!

Yes, I know that the books tell you to never play a hand like that, but in this situation you can represent strength with a raise. Your opponents appear weak and they don't know you have garbage in the hole, so chances are you'll win the hand right then and there.

Let's look at another example; this one from a Texas hold'em game. Everyone has folded to you in last position, and you're dealt the worst hand in hold'em: 7-2 offsuit. Probably 98 percent of the time I'd suggest folding this junk and waiting for a better situation. Unless, of course, you know that the two players in the blinds are conservative types who operate very predictably.

In this case, you can raise with any two cards. Now, this is important because you won't be playing your hand, you'll be playing theirs.

If you do raise, chances are the blinds will both fold. That would be the most desired result, but even if they don't, you aren't necessarily out of the hand.

Suppose the big blind calls your raise and the flop comes A♠9♣4♦. If the conservative player in the big blind doesn't have the ace, he'll probably check to you. Despite the fact that you have nothing at all, you should still bet on the flop.

If your opponent calls the bet, or, worse, raises, then you'll abort mission. But what will happen more often than not is that he'll fold if he doesn't have the pair of aces.

That's not the only way you can win the pot; you could hit the flop yourself. Sure, 7-2 is a really poor hand, and difficult to hit, but you might just get lucky and flop a pair, two pair, or even three of a kind.

While playing trash hands isn't something you'll ever *have* to do, if you want to reach the next level of poker thinking, it's something you'll eventually *have* to try. So, go ahead and add this play to your arsenal.

Most beginning players are focused on, "What do I have?" The next step from there is, "What does my opponent have?" The third step, and the one that helps explain why in the world Gus Hansen always seems to have a junk hand, is "What does my opponent think I have?"

Gus is a brilliant poker professional and is fully aware that he's perceived as a garbage collector. Since he understands the way opponents view him, he takes full advantage of that and gets paid handsomely when he hits his strong hands.

There is a method to this kind of perceived madness. Don't judge an opponent by the garbage he plays. Instead, focus on *how* he plays these trashy hands, and recycle that information for later in the game.

22.

Calling with the Worse Hand

Situations will sometimes arise at the poker table when you just know that your opponent has you beat, but you should still call anyway. A perfect example occurred at the 2006 National Heads-Up Poker Championship in a hand between me and my good friend, poker professional, Evelyn Ng.

In the hand, Evelyn raised to $1,200 before the flop, and I called with J♠9♠. The flop came J♦4♥3♦, and I checked. Evelyn bet $1,600. At that point, she was ahead in the match, and I only had $12,600 in chips left.

Finally, after much thought, I decided to go all-in hoping that she couldn't beat my pair of jacks. She thought about calling for quite some time but eventually folded the 7♦4♦.

On the surface, it might seem like Evelyn made the right decision. After all, I had a pair of jacks and she only had a pair of fours. With poker, though, as I hope you'll learn from me, there is often more to it than hand strength alone.

First, let's look at the odds of her hand against mine.

Since she could catch a 4, a 7, or a diamond, to win the pot, her hand was actually the slight favorite at 51 percent. In fact, the only hands that she wouldn't be favored against would be two pair or three of a kind. Even against trip jacks, she would still win the pot almost 30 percent of the time.

That's not the only thing she had to ponder.

Evelyn was faced with a bet of $11,000, but with what was already put in before the flop, as well as the bet she made on the flop, she'd have to risk $11,000 to win $16,600. She was even money to win the pot, but the pot was laying her approximately 3 to 2 odds ($16,600/$11,000). Also, she had to consider that this was an opportunity to end the match.

It's important to note that certain draws are so powerful that they can actually be the favorite to win the pot.

For example, if you hold 5♥6♥ and the flop came 6♦7♥8♥, you'd be the favorite to win the pot—even against pocket aces! In fact, you'd be a substantial favorite, improving to the winning hand about 64 percent of the time.

There's a rule you can use to help figure out whether or not your drawing hand is a favorite against an opponent.

The rule: With the turn and river cards yet to come, if there are thirteen cards that will improve your hand to the winner, then you're a very small underdog. If fourteen cards can make your hand, you'll be just about even money to win.

Here's a hand example I recently analyzed.

Player A's cards:

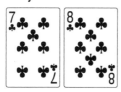

Player B's cards:

The flop:

Player A had thirteen cards to improve his hand (eight clubs, two sevens, and three eights). His hand will win the pot 47 percent of the time.

Now, change the card in Player B's hand from the 2♣ to the 2♥, and Player A actually goes from an underdog to a very slight favorite, winning the pot 50.1 percent of the time. Even more enticing, in a hand where Player A has fifteen outs, he'd be more than a 56 percent favorite.

You don't need a PhD in mathematics to play poker, but it will serve you well to remember these odds.

This knowledge becomes increasingly important when playing in no-limit hold'em tournaments. An extreme example would be a situation where a player has gone all-in, and you're the big blind with a pitiful hand like 3-2 offsuit.

You know for certain that your opponent has you beat, but that doesn't necessarily mean that you should fold. First, calculate the pot odds you're getting. Then, assess your chances of winning by counting your outs.

Here's a final example: You have $400 in the big blind, and an opponent goes all-in for $700. So, the bet facing you is only $300 more. Including the small blind, you'd be risking $300 to win $1,300. That's over 4 to 1 pot odds and is very favorable. Even if your opponent has a powerful hand like A-K, you'd still get lucky and win the pot 34 percent of the time.

You won't win at poker by simply playing good hands. In order to reach that next level, you need to change the way you think about the game. Don't always be concerned with whether or not you have the best hand. Instead, focus on whether or not the pot odds dictate that you should play the hand.

23.

Dangerous Hands to Play, Dangerous Hands to Own

Danger is all around you at the poker table.

The trick to becoming a successful poker player is learning how to avoid these dangerous traps, while striking fear into your opponents by playing some tricky hands.

Dangerous Hands to Play

The worst type of hand you can be dealt when playing Texas hold'em is one that seems to be too good to fold, but isn't good enough to raise with. Sure, it's easy to know that you should raise with pocket aces and fold a 7-2 offsuit, but hands like K-J offsuit can often cause you real problems.

While it's obvious that high cards are better than low cards, in most no-limit hold'em situations, the little cards often have a better risk/reward ratio.

The potential problem with trouble hands like K-J, A-J, Q-J, or even K-Q, is that when you flop a pair with them you'll often have kicker trouble. Too often, when you call a raise with a hand like K-Q you'll be up against A-K, or maybe even A-A or K-K.

If you're in there with K-Q and the flop comes Q-6-2, you'll have what appears to be a really strong hand. The problem, though, is that if someone decides to play against you after the flop, there is a good chance you're going to get beat.

The bottom line is clear: If you were to play a big pot on that flop, for all of your money, chances are that you are walking into a set (trip deuces, sixes, or queens), an A-Q, a pair of kings, or a pair of aces.

Generally speaking, these trouble hands often win small pots when no one else hits the flop, and lose monster pots when they run into a better hand. Why? Because it's really difficult to fold such a seemingly strong hand after a flop like that.

Now don't get me wrong. I'm not recommending that you never play a hand like K-Q or A-J, but always remember, that when you do, you need to proceed cautiously. Don't get married to your top pair if a quality opponent is pushing the betting hard.

Dangerous Hands to Own

Now, compare the previous examples to playing a hand like a pocket pair of fours. This hand is much easier to work with. Either you hit the flop big, by landing three of a kind, or you have a hand with very little value.

Let's look at another example. You call a raise with 4-4 from late position, from a player who you suspect has a strong hand, maybe even A-A. You aren't calling because you think your little pair is the best hand, but you are doing so because of the potential to win a big pot.

Let's say the flop now comes J♠4♣2♦. Or, in other words, Gin baby!

If your opponent did in fact start with a hand like A-A, K-K, or Q-Q, chances are you'll be able to win his whole stack if you bet it right. Had the flop come something like J-9-8, then you can safely fold your pair of fours without risking another chip. As you can see, it's a minor risk in relation to the big payday a small pair might offer you.

There is one last group of hands that you might want to add to your repertoire—playing small-suited connectors like 7-6. These hands can be a little trickier than small pairs, but you'll be able to connect with them more often. The same principle holds true with these little cards as with the little pairs. Get to the flop cheaply if you can and get out if you don't improve.

Let's look at one final example. You call a raise with 6-7 of hearts and the flop comes 6-6-2. If your opponent has a big overpair, you might be able to win all of his chips, because he may not believe that you'd call a raise with a 6 in your hand.

The key difference between dangerous hands to play and dangerous hands to own is that it's easy to get away from the latter, but it's often very difficult to avoid getting trapped with a risky hand like top pair.

Be the dangerous player—not the player in danger.

24.

Playing on a Short Stack

When playing in a poker tournament you'll often find yourself in situations where you're short-stacked in relation to the blinds. This can happen for a number of reasons. Maybe you've lost a big hand, or perhaps the cards just haven't been coming for you.

Whatever the cause, you have limited options, but you *do* have options.

Too often I see players go all-in with garbage hands, essentially giving up, since they are short-stacked. Well, would you believe that World Series of Poker champion Jack Strauss, actually came back to win the main event after being down to just one measly chip?

The old adage, "A chip and a chair," is a motto to live by.

Rather than just giving up and throwing your chips in foolishly, here are some strategies to get you back into the game and on the right track when you're short-stacked.

1. Wait for a decent hand.

Now is not the time to try and see a lot of flops with weak

hands. You need to look for a hand that plays well, *hot and cold*; meaning, one that has a good chance of being the best hand before the flop. While hands like 6-5 suited are enticing, they obviously don't do very well hot and cold. However, hands like A-10 or K-Q would have a very good chance to win if you were lucky enough to hit a pair.

2. Go all-in.

When you're short-stacked you have limited weapons, so when you do decide to play a hand, go all or nothing and bet everything you have left. If nobody calls, you'll win the blinds and antes which will help you claw your way back to respectability. In fact, when playing short-stacked, your goal should be to win those blinds and antes.

3. Be the first player to enter the pot.

It's much better to be the first one into the pot when you play as a short stack. If someone has already raised in front of you, and then you go all-in, the chances that they'll call your bet increase. You simply wouldn't have enough chips to scare them off.

Since your goal as a short stack is to attack the blinds and antes, logic dictates that if someone else has already shown interest in seeing the flop, it will be more difficult to get them to fold if you go all-in.

4. Avoid the big stacks.

Unless you have a premium starting hand, avoid going after the blind of a player who has a big stack of chips. He's more likely to defend his blind since your puny short stack won't do a lot of damage to him. Instead, you want to target other short stacks and average-sized stacks. Players with average stacks can't be as careless with their chips, so it will be easier to take their blinds.

5. Don't give up.

Just remember Jack Strauss. He became a World Champion when it looked like there was no way he could win another hand let alone the whole championship.

You have to stay positive, dig deep and try to claw your way back into the tournament. Too many players give up, inevitably saying something like, "I didn't have a choice. I had no chips anyway."

Well, you always have a choice, and the decisions you make as a short stack aren't insignificant at all. In fact, they are critical.

Here are a couple of final thoughts on the topic.

It's important to figure out just how short your stack is. If your stack is just below average and the blinds are relatively small, there is no real need for drastic adjustments to your strategy. However, if you find yourself with just one big blind left, you can't afford to wait too long for a hand to play. You'll have to lower your starting hand requirements significantly and hope for the best.

The last thing you want to do is ante yourself to death. When your stack becomes excessively short, hands like Q-7 suited or A-5 offsuit are clearly playable. Go ahead and toss all of your remaining chips into the pot.

And keep your fingers crossed.

25.

Controlling the Table with a Big Stack

There is nothing more exciting than having a monster-sized stack in a no-limit hold'em tournament. With a big pile of chips, there are so many ways you can use them to gather even more. Sheer brute aggression is one, but that approach can also jeopardize your stack if you aren't being careful.

You see, while you want to use a big stack to bully the table, it's equally important to protect your chips so that you can continue to be the dominant force. If you're reckless with your chips and lose a big pot, it will greatly limit the weapons that you have in your arsenal.

Here are six things to think about the next time you're sitting on a big stack in a tournament.

1. Attack the short stacks.

When players are down to very few chips, their options are severely limited. They're forced to wait for any decent hand and then move all-in.

In the meantime, push them around with your big stack,

since, even if they do play with you, the damage to your chip fortress would be minimal.

When there are short stacks in the blinds, be very aggressive and raise with a wide variety of hands. Understand, it's not really all that important how strong your cards are. What matters is whether or not your opponents can find a hand strong enough to stand up to yours.

2. Avoid the big stacks.

The last thing you want to do is tangle with another player who also has a monster stack, unless of course you have a premium hand. The targets that you should be bluffing at are the chip-challenged opponents that can't hurt you too badly. Remember, you always want to protect your big stack, so when you're up against a player that could cripple your stack, proceed with caution. Don't get involved unless you have a quality hand.

3. Don't play big pots.

One way to protect your stack is to avoid playing big pots in marginal situations. Your goal is to increase your chip count slowly by avoiding major risks. So, in situations where you aren't totally sure that you have the best hand, play cautiously. Continue to stay aggressive in small pots, but don't risk a large percentage of your chips unless you have the nuts or close to it.

4. Be creative.

One of the luxuries of having a big stack is that you can use every poker trick in the book: slowplaying, trapping, bluffing, semibluffing and a host of others. While you want to be aggressive throughout, having a big stack affords you opportunities to mix it up, try out new tactics, and play hands deceptively.

When your opponents think they have you all figured

out, it's time to throw them a curveball and play a hand in an uncharacteristic style. This will be great for your table image as it makes you an unpredictable player that is tough to put on a hand.

5. Strike fear in your opponents.

You want to be an imposing figure at the table when you're a big stack. Your opponents should fear you whether you're betting, sitting in the big blind or haven't even acted yet. When they're afraid to play with you, you'll control the table.

6. Be a constant presence.

Let opponents know that you're there to play, not to sit on your stack. Use your mouth, but don't be rude, cocky, or annoying. You need your competitors to believe that you are on a mission. That alone will make you a pain in everyone's side. Cultivate that relentlessly aggressive image and opponents will be convinced that you'll play that way all day long. If players fear you, they'll often throw away hands they might otherwise raise you with.

Following these six strategy tips will help your stack grow higher and lead you to more final tables.

26.

Playing Fast, Playing Slow

When it comes to the concept of *fastplaying* versus *slowplaying* in poker, it really doesn't matter what specific game you're talking about.

It is important, however, to understand that different forms of poker require unique approaches and strategies. So, while it might be correct to habitually slowplay in a game like seven-card stud high-low, it might end up being a huge mistake in limit Texas hold'em.

In fact, limit hold'em is the one game where being an all-out, fast, aggressive maniac is most rewarded. On top of that, if you happen to be playing *short-handed* (six or less players), I'd suggest putting on your seatbelt!

Limit hold'em simply isn't designed to reward slowplay. That's not to say you should never suck opponents into a pot, but the situations where it's correct to do so are rare. Since it's so easy for a marginal hand to be outdrawn in a limit game, it's important to bet and raise with these types of hands to narrow down the field and thus increase your chances of winning the pot.

The only time you might want to slowplay in limit hold'em is when you have an almost unbeatable hand and you feel as though betting will scare opponents away. For example, you have A♥7♥ and the flop comes K♥6♥3♥. This is a decent time to slowplay your hand, as it's highly unlikely that someone will beat you on the turn or river.

The best limit hold'em players all have one thing in common; they pound, pound and pound, keeping it in high gear, fastplaying most of the way. Follow their lead and play your hands fast and aggressive.

While limit poker is a game of brute force, no-limit requires more finesse, trapping skills and creativity. No-limit rewards players like two-time World Champion Johnny Chan, who uses sly betting patterns to feign weakness, trap opponents, and break them before they even know what hit them.

It's no coincidence that Chan earned the nickname, "The Oriental Sand Trap." Johnny is a master of using slowplay. That moniker is well represented in the film *Rounders*. In it, Johnny flops the nut straight against Erik Seidel, and then allows Seidel to hang himself without Chan ever making a bet. All he does is provide the rope.

If you're considering adding slow play to your repertoire, there are a few simple rules you should follow.

Find the right opponent.

The best type of opponent to slowplay against is the one who plays very aggressively and bluffs a lot. The player that will see your check as a sign of weakness and will look to take the pot away from you is a great target. Slowplaying against a timid player is much less effective.

Have a monster hand.

In order to justify slowplaying, you must hold a very strong hand. One pair, even if it's A-A or K-K, is still a marginal hand after the flop is dealt. Slowplay a hand like that and you'll often find that you're only trapping yourself into losing a monster pot.

Have a plan.

Don't just automatically slowplay a nut flush on the flop for the sake of using the ploy. Always think about how to maximize your profit in the hand, too. So, depending on the table action, don't count out fastplaying the nuts on the flop. In the right situation, fastplay might garner even more action than slowplay.

Avoid predictability.

If you always slowplay with monster hands, opponents will quickly notice, and your plan will be foiled. Be conscious of the fact that you must mix it up. Sometimes bet the flop when you have a full house; other times, check, looking for the slowplay opportunity.

Also remember this: Never underestimate how perceptive your opponents are. They're always trying to figure you out, so don't make it easy on them.

Mixing up fastplay and slowplay will keep the guessers guessing.

27.

Three Dangerous Flops

Most of the difficult decisions you'll face in a typical Texas hold'em poker hand will come after the flop. It's easy enough to figure out what a good hand is before the flop, and how you should play it, but there are many more variables to consider after the flop. Once those three community cards are dealt, many more possibilities exist.

Here are three particularly dangerous flops along with some advice on how you should proceed.

The Paired Flop

A paired flop can either be a really good discovery for you, or the flop of death. Let's say you start with a pair of kings, and the flop comes Q♥7♠7♣. In this situation you have two pair, kings and sevens.

Obviously, if nobody has a 7 in their hand, you are in excellent shape (unless one of your opponents started with pocket queens or pocket aces). Since there are no draws on the board, it appears to be a pretty straightforward situation.

But what if someone raises you?

Your beautiful pair of kings might be up against a hand like A-Q. Or, you could easily be drawing to one of only two remaining kings left in the deck in the event that your opponent has the trip sevens.

The best way to approach a flop like this with an overpair is to go ahead and bet, but if you receive any resistance, proceed with caution. Don't go crazy by raising and reraising. Be content to just call the hand down and hope your opponent has queens rather than the dreaded three sevens.

The Coordinated Flop

A coordinated flop is one where there is a three card straight present, something like Q-10-8. Let's say you hold a pair of aces, and there are three callers. A flop like that is extremely dangerous since it hits a range of cards with which your opponents might call. Hands like Q-J, Q-10, J-9, 8-8 are all cards that your competitors could feasibly be holding.

While three out of the four hands already have your aces beat (two pair, a straight, and three of a kind), even the first hand, Q-J, isn't too far behind your pocket bullets. If a 9, J or Q arrives on the turn or river, he'll beat you too. In fact, your aces are only a 2 to 1 favorite over the Q-J on that flop.

The more players that are in the pot, preflop, the more often a big pair ends up as a loser. The goal is to try narrowing the field by raising aggressively on the flop and then, if the turn card is a bad one (8, 9, 10, J, Q, K), it's time to play very cautiously, even if that means folding.

The Flushed Flop

When the flop comes with three of the same suit, playing an overpair, without holding one of the suit, can be very tricky.

Let's say you start with J♣J♠, and the flop is 8♥6♥2♥. While you do have a nice overpair, one more heart on the turn and your strong pocket jacks will likely be meaningless.

The best way to approach a hand like this is to bet the flop, but don't get too aggressive by raising. You could, of course, raise all you want on the flop, but if someone has a heart in their hand, chances are he's going to call you anyway.

You need to understand that it's better to play cautiously on the flop, since there are still two cards to come. If a safe card comes on the turn, that's when you might want to punish your opponent who is drawing to a flush.

Now, if there are several players in the pot, you might even be better off folding right away on the flop. With six callers before the flop, it stands to reason that there is a decent chance one of your opponents may have hit their flush on the flop. If it's bet and raised in front of you, I would definitely suggest folding.

28.

Don't Get Married to Your Aces

When playing Texas hold'em there is nothing sweeter than looking down at a beautiful pair of rockets, bullets, American Airlines, the nuts, or whatever you want to call a pocket pair of aces.

Just be careful with them.

While they're definitely the best starting hand you can get, they could come with significant problems, especially if you fall deeply in love with them, and especially in no-limit Texas hold'em.

Here's the problem. Many players have a tough time believing that pocket aces could ever lose. It happens, all right, happens to everybody. In fact, even 7-2 offsuit will beat aces about 12.5 percent of the time.

The scariest bullet busters are suited connectors and small pairs. A hand like 7-6 suited will beat aces an astounding 23 percent of the time, while a lowly pair of deuces will crack aces about 13.5 percent of the time. Though 13.5 percent may not seem like all that much, it ends up becoming very significant when you add betting to the mix.

Let's say, for example, you raise before the flop with your aces, and your opponent calls you with 2-2. If the flop comes a **rainbow** J-6-2, that is, cards of all different suits, your pair of aces are in for some big trouble. It's tough to just throw the hand away on such a ragged flop, which is exactly what makes playing a hand like wired deuces so alluring for an opponent.

The 2-2 is so much easier to play. If you don't catch a third deuce on the flop, you can simply dump your hand and wait for the next opportunity.

That's not nearly as easy to do that when you have A-A.

No-limit Texas hold'em specifically is a game of *implied odds*, meaning that you are looking to make small investments early in the hand in the hopes that it will pay off big time later on.

Similar to buying blue chip stocks on Wall Street, pocket aces are a solid bet. But keep in mind that the stock market can tank at any moment, just like your pair of aces.

Compare that to the 2-2, a penny stock hand, where your modest investment with marginal risk might end up as a home run.

The truly great players recognize the problem with playing big pairs like A-A, K-K, and Q-Q and make the necessary adjustments. Rather than over value their big pairs, they proceed cautiously in the face of danger.

If, for example, a flop comes 6-7-8 and he has A-A, a top player wouldn't be so quick to go all-in, fearing a possible straight, trips, or even two pair. He may choose to just call an opponent's bet. If the heat becomes too strong, he'd seriously consider folding the hand to avoid a situation where he may have been doomed to go broke.

A novice player might complain about his bad luck when his pocket aces lose to an opponent who played 10-9. Oftentimes, it wasn't the rookie's luck that lost him all of his money. It was his inability to recognize the danger in that flop and the potential for losing all of his chips.

Take this lesson to heart and your playing strategy is born.

If you face an opponent who isn't capable of folding big pairs after the flop, it makes sense to play him with weaker hands. Even though you are fully aware that he likely has a premium hand, it's still a solid play.

In fact, with a hand like 3-3, 4-4, or 6-5 suited, that's precisely what you want him to have. That way, if you are lucky enough to hit a monster flop, you'll have that poor sucker on the ropes, desperately hoping for a miracle ace to save him.

That's exactly what great players will attempt to do against a novice. They'll try to make a small investment with some off-the-wall hands hoping to catch a big flop and take the rookie for all of his chips.

When you see someone like Gus Hansen playing on television, or myself for that matter, playing all kinds of hands that you aren't *supposed* to play, remember that there is method to the madness.

We just happen to like gambling on penny stocks with big upside potential.

29.

Where To Sit at the Poker Table?

While this may seem rather silly to some, there is actually merit to the question, "Where is the best place to sit at a poker table?"

No, I'm not talking about closest to the bathroom or to the fridge. I'm talking about where the best place is for you to sit at the poker table in relation to certain types of players.

If you've played poker at all, you know that people approach the game in different ways—some by the seat of their pants, others very carefully. You have experienced players and novices, aggressive types and conservative competitors. Eventually you'll meet them all at the poker table, and knowing which seat offers you the best chance for winning against whoever you might face can only improve your game.

There is a general rule when picking your seat that you should always abide by. You want the most difficult players on your right. Here's where you should try to be for each type of player.

1. Conservative or tight players.

These rocks are no real threat to you, so, abiding by the general rule, you shouldn't really care all that much where they sit. Ideally, though, you'd want these players to your left so that you can pick on their blinds. If they happen to play with you when you've entered the pot, you can be sure they have a strong hand. Act accordingly. That wouldn't always be true with the next group of players.

2. Aggressive players.

These are the players that you need to worry about. An aggressive player on your left means you're somewhat handcuffed. You have to play a little more conservatively now because having that monster behind you means you don't know what he'll do until after you've acted.

You'll always prefer the aggressive players on your right so that you can keep an eye on them and then spank them when they get out of line! Basically, you'll be able to use your position to exploit the aggressive player.

If you have a seating choice, when facing both an aggressive and a conservative player, sit right between them with the tighter player on your left.

Things get a bit trickier when you're figuring out where to sit when playing either a novice or an experienced player, since you'll want both of them on your right to some degree.

3. Novice players.

If you are playing with a rookie, chances are he's going to make a lot of mistakes, and you want to be in there when he does. So by sitting on his left you'll have the opportunity to see whether or not he enters the pot. Since you'll have position on him you can manipulate the novice much easier and force him into even more mistakes.

According to the general rule, you'll want players you

worry about on your right, but in this case you aren't worried about the novice since you can control or exploit him better if you sit on his left.

4. Experienced players.

Well this obviously depends on how good the experienced players are, but generally these competitors surprise you less often than a novice player. They will most likely play fundamentally sound, which, while more predictable, doesn't necessarily make it easier for you. You'll want a tough, aggressive experienced player sitting on your right. But against a more conservative experienced player, you'd prefer him on your left rather than the easily exploitable novice.

You're not always going to be able to pick your seat, especially in a tournament, so it's important to know how to play against both novice and aggressive opponents when they are seated to your left.

When the novice is on your left, all that really means is you'll have less opportunities to exploit him, but you don't need to make any major strategy adjustments.

With the aggressive player on your left, however, you need to make significant strategy adjustments. You really need to respect the fact that position is power, and since this competitor has it, you must concede your relative weakness a little bit and play accordingly.

From time to time, look to set traps for the aggressive player by slowplaying strong hands. This should help keep him from breathing down your neck on a regular basis. Other than that, just tighten up a little bit and wait for a better situation to arise—like maybe, switching seats!

30.

The Check-Raise

Whether you're playing limit hold'em, seven-card stud, Omaha, or even no-limit hold'em, the *check-raise* can be a deadly weapon when used properly.

Check-raising, in a nutshell, is a play in which you pass your turn by not betting. That's the *check*, and it should suggest, since you didn't want to bet, that you don't have a strong hand. Once you check, and another player bets, you pounce out of the high grass with the *raise*.

It's obviously a powerful tool and sometimes a controversial one.

In some home games, the check-raise is outlawed entirely because of its deceptive nature. Come on now, we're playing poker here!

While the play has always had a negative connotation attached to it, I'm here to tell you that the check-raise is your friend.

There should never be rules that suggest you can't bluff or use deception to maximize your profit. It's all part of the game. If you and your friends play with a no check-raising rule, all you're doing is making the game less interesting and more robotic.

The key thing about the check-raise is that it helps to neutralize a positional disadvantage. While you should understand that it's better to act last, the check-raise is a weapon that can help an out-of-position player defend himself.

Let's say, for example, that you're playing in a no-limit game where check-raising isn't allowed. You find yourself heads-up against an opponent on the river and check to him. Obviously, your opponent is in a very powerful position. He can bet whatever amount he wants without fear of a check-raise. That puts you, the out-of-position player, at an unfair disadvantage.

Now, suppose you're in the exact same situation, but this time check-raising is allowed. Once you check on the river, your opponent now must think twice about betting a marginal hand. He'd have to ask himself, "Is he playing possum and waiting to check-raise me?"

Adding that element of fear helps shift a degree of power back to the player sitting out of position. It's still much better to be in position, mind you, but with the check-raise option available, it makes it a much more level playing field.

The check-raise is especially effective against aggressive opponents who often bet when someone shows weakness by checking. An aggressive player always looks to steal pots; so, by checking to him, you let him bluff off his money before smacking him back with a raise.

Here are six ways the check-raise will help you to improve your game:

1. It neutralizes the positional disadvantage.

Without the use of the check-raise, you're forced to play even more conservatively when out of position.

2. It allows you to trap aggressive opponents for extra bets.

Against aggressive competitors, you'll often be able to win extra bets when they try to steal the pot after you've checked.

3. It adds deception to your game.

Check-raising is an excellent way to mix up your game and become less predictable. Sometimes you'll check with a strong hand, while other times you'll bet right out. The check-raise, or lack of it, will keep them guessing.

4. It makes your opponents think twice about betting after you've checked.

Once your opponents know that you're capable of raising after you've checked, it will often fool them into checking the best hand behind you, which often earns you a valuable free card.

5. It helps you to knock players out of the pot.

In situations where you want to narrow down the field, a check-raise can help you force an opponent to fold a hand that he'd likely call for one bet, but would fold for two bets.

6. It gives you another bluffing option.

Since the check-raise is often seen as a powerful ploy played with a powerful hand, you can also use it as a sophisticated bluff against thinking opponents.

The check-raise just makes poker more fun. So don't take it personally when a friend traps you with a check-raise. It's all part of the game.

31.

Table Position

People often ask me the question, "How do you play K-J offsuit?" My answer is always the same: "It depends."

The most important consideration when deciding how to play any poker hand, aside from the strength of the hand, is your position at the table.

Position can be broken down into three categories: early, middle, and late. At a nine-handed table, the first three seats to the left of the button are considered **early position**. The next three are **middle position**, and the last two seats, as well as the player on the dealer button, are **late position**.

The absolute best position to enter a pot from is that final dealer spot. When you play a hand from the button you have the advantage of seeing all of your opponents' actions before deciding what you want to do, and you get to keep that deadly weapon throughout the entire hand.

How cool is that?

Now just for a second let's pretend that you aren't playing poker, but instead you're seated at a blackjack table. In blackjack, the dealer immediately has a huge advantage because you have to act, hit or stand, before he does.

Let's say you're dealt 7-6 for a 13 and the dealer is showing an 8. Well, any book will tell you that you need to hit on a 13 against an 8. So you tap the table and ask for a card and it's a big fat king. Busted!

The dealer then turns over his concealed card and reveals a 5, meaning that he started with the same 13 that you did. One big difference is that the dealer didn't have to run the gauntlet and risk busting like you just did. Add to that the fact that if your 13 improved to a 17 the dealer would still have an opportunity to beat you if he drew a 5, 6, 7, or an 8.

Okay, so why am I discussing blackjack in a poker book?

It's because similar principles hold true when factoring in your position at the poker table. In Texas hold'em, the most popular form of poker in the world, you must remember that your two-card starting hand will miss the flop more often than it will hit. There are going to be many situations where the pot is up for grabs, and the first person to bet at it will likely pick it up.

Having position in these types of situations is a great benefit.

Let's say you have one other player in the pot with you, and you have that precious dealer button. The flop comes A♣ J♠ 4♦ and your hand is 10♥ 8♥.

It doesn't take a rocket scientist to figure out that the flop completely missed your hand. Since we know that more often than not the flop will miss your opponent's hand, too, you may still be able to pick up this pot because you are in the power position.

If your opponent checks on the flop, you can simply bet right there as a bluff. If he doesn't have the ace, and has any poker sense at all, he'll fold his hand—making you the winner.

Now if your opponent bets right out on the flop, you

can safely fold your hand and save the bluff bet you were planning.

The only real equalizer to someone having position on you is the deadly check-raise. Using this tactic, an opponent checks to you with a strong hand, trying to conceal it, and then pounces on your bet with a big raise. It's never a good feeling when that situation occurs, but it happens to everyone sooner or later.

While the check-raise play definitely offsets some of the button's edge, it's also very risky and can be expensive. For a check-raise to work, you have to know, or have a very strong suspicion, that your opponent, will, in fact bet if you check. If he doesn't bet, then you've just given him a free card that might just cost you the pot.

So knowing how important position is to your overall success, it makes sense to play more conservatively when seated in an early position and more aggressively when in a late position. And if you decide to play a hand from an early position, it had better be a premium hand.

On the button? That's where you can really be creative, stretch your starting hand requirements, and play with power.

32.

Limit Hold'em Tactics in No-Limit Hold'em Games

Don't be a one-trick pony. Learning how to play more than just no-limit Texas hold'em will actually make you a better overall poker player, and, ironically, will make you a better no-limit hold'em player as well.

Limit and no-limit hold'em are played very differently, but that doesn't mean that you can't use some limit tactics in no-limit. In fact, there are several poker weapons that are considered limit plays, but when used correctly are very effective in the game of no-limit.

Let's look at two of these plays and how they relate to each game.

Betting the flop

In limit hold'em, it's common practice for a player who raises before the flop to bet at least once more on the flop. The goal is to quickly pick up the pot in the hope that your opponents miss with the first community cards.

Well, this is also an effective weapon in no-limit hold'em. However, there are a few important differences.

Betting the flop in no-limit will win you the pot more often, but you'll usually be risking more money. Because limit betting is structured, in a $10/$20 limit hold'em game, it will only cost you $10 to try and steal the pot. If the bet doesn't work, the damage is minimal.

In no-limit, though, the pain could be much more severe. Since you can bet all of your chips at any time, you're also risking your entire stack if you push it all-in on the wrong flop.

To avoid that catastrophe, take a lesson from successful limit players.

Rather than bet the whole pot in a no-limit game, bet anywhere from one-third to one-half of the pot. A bet of half the pot will generally have the same effect as a pot-sized bet, and it will cost you much less if the bluff doesn't work.

Three-betting before the flop

When you watch high-stakes limit hold'em poker, you'll often see a preflop raise, followed by a reraise. Then, the pot is generally played heads-up, with the player who put in the last raise before the flop taking the lead.

This gives the three-bettor control of the hand and allows him to represent strength. If his opponent misses the flop, the aggressor can often take the pot away with another bet on the flop. This tactic works even better when the aggressor also has position.

Here's an example of how this might work in limit hold'em.

Player A raises with 7-7, and Player B decides to reraise from the button with 5-5. The flop comes A-K-9. Player A checks. Player B bets with position. Now, all Player A can do is fold due to the scary board, thus allowing Player B to win the pot with a weaker hand.

This play works well in no-limit hold'em, too, albeit in a very different form.

When a player makes it three bets in limit hold'em, the first raiser will always call one more bet to see the flop. That's not true in no-limit.

You can raise more than just one bet in no-limit, so you can actually force your opponent to fold before the flop.

Let's look at another example, but now in a no-limit game.

The blinds are $10/$20, and Player A raises to $60 with pocket sevens. This time, Player B, sitting on the button with A-K, reraises to $200. Player A now has a very difficult decision to make. If he decides to call and see the flop, he'll likely fold to another forceful bet unless he catches his third seven.

If the flop comes something like Q-10-4, Player A will check, and player B might bet, say, $300. There is almost no way that Player A can call that bet.

The key difference between limit and no-limit hold'em is the level of aggressive play employed on the flop.

Because it's far riskier to bet after the flop, no-limit players tend to play the board more carefully. By so doing, they're essentially giving up on pots that they could often win with a bet.

So, as if you were playing in a limit game, keep your no-limit pots small by lowering your bet sizes. This will reduce the risk associated with playing the perilous game of no-limit hold'em.

33.

Setting Up a Bluff

One of the biggest mistakes I see novice players make is that they bluff in situations when it couldn't possibly work.

I cannot tell you how many times I've heard this excuse: "Well I had to try. I couldn't win if I didn't try to bluff." To that I say, "Did you ever think that maybe you couldn't have won anyway?"

Wasted, desperation bluffs will drain your bankroll faster than Dracula would necks at a blood drive.

There is an easy solution—to the poker problem, anyway.

You have to set up a bluff by thoroughly thinking it through early in the hand. Playing an effective bluff is similar to telling an elaborate lie.

For example, let's say you call your boss to let him know you can't come to work because you're in bed with the flu. But, in fact, you aren't home at all and are calling him from your swanky hotel room in Vegas.

The first thing your boss is going to look for is a hole in your story. In this case, when his caller ID comes up with the 702 area code, how are you going to explain that one?

"I thought you were sick in bed with the flu? What's up with the 702 area code?"

Your response would undoubtedly be something lame, like, "Errr, umm. I dunno."

Your bluff didn't make sense because you didn't set it up right. The supposed fact you presented in your story didn't make any sense at all. You needed to tell a more believable story and back it up with some action that didn't contradict what you were saying—like *69ing yourself to block your caller ID!

Okay then, let's take a look at how all of this bluffing relates to playing a hand of poker.

In a $5/$10 Texas hold'em game, holding 10♥J♥, you raise before the flop, and one player calls your bet. The flop comes K♥9♥4♦, and you bet $5 with your flush and straight draw. Your opponent raises you another $5 and you call.

The turn card is the 7♦ and you check to your opponent who bets $10. You, of course, call the bet. Now the river card comes 2♣, or in poker terms—a big fat brick!

This is simply not the time or place to attempt a bluff.

You certainly can't win if you check, but what I'm trying to explain is that you aren't going to win if you bet, either. Your bet would make no sense. It would be a meaningless bluff. Don't do it.

Ask yourself this question: What junk am I trying to peddle by betting when the 2♣ comes on the river?

If your opponent has anything at all, he is going to call your bluff in a heartbeat. Because you played the hand so cautiously up until the river card, it's now too late to try and represent a strong hand. The only story you've told with your betting action is that you don't have a very good hand.

So how *do* you make a bluff work?

It's critical that you set up the bluff early in the hand. Play it from the start in such a way that your opponents might actually think you have very strong cards. In the preceding scenario, there would have been several ways to do that:

1. Re-raise the bet on the flop.

2. Check-raise the bet on the flop.

3. Check-raise the bet on the turn.

Had you acted in any of these ways, and took control of the hand early, your river bet would have looked like it made sense.

One of the great things about poker is that there are so many variables and so many ways to play different situations. If you choose to play a bluff, great, just set it up from the start. Just as importantly, eliminate those desperate river card bluffs and you'll erase a huge weakness in your game.

34.

The Top 10 Myths About Poker

When you've been around poker for as long as I have, you've heard every theory, rumor, and falsehood about the game. Poker is indeed full of myths, and here are some of the big ones.

1. Poker is illegal.

Nothing could be further from the truth. In fact, the U.S. government recognizes poker as a game of skill. Yes, there might be jurisdictions where playing poker for money is illegal, but there is nothing at all illegal about playing poker with friends, or even playing poker for a living.

2. It takes several years to learn.

It's not true, at least not anymore. Today, thanks to people like Doyle Brunson, who wrote *Super System*, it's easier than ever to learn how to play poker at a competitive level. There are also numerous books, software, DVDs, and other teaching tools available.

3. Poker is all about bluffing.

No, it's not. In fact, that's one of the big mistakes novice players make when they start out in poker. Professionals win by getting full value for their strong hands, while minimizing their losses on losing hands. Bluffing is a tool that should be used sporadically, making it that much more effective.

4. It's a man's game.

Hardly. We are seeing more and more women—amateurs and professionals alike—playing these days. One of the world's best players, Jennifer Harman, is a regular winner in the world's biggest cash game against the likes of poker professionals Chip Reese and Phil Ivey.

5. Online poker is rigged.

Some people have a tendency to blame anyone but themselves. Before the arrival of online poker, complainers blamed the casino dealer for their bad luck. Online poker has become the new victim of abuse from players who would rather blame their computer than their lack of poker skills.

6. Poker is gambling and you have to gamble to make it fun.

Too often, poker and gambling are considered to be synonymous. Yes, poker is a game and, yes, you can gamble at it. But you can also gamble on Monopoly, Hop Scotch, or even the flip of a coin. I know, because I've made wagers on all of the above!

7. No-limit hold'em is the most skillful form of poker.

There is actually a form of poker that requires even more skill: pot-limit hold'em. This game gives solid players a bigger advantage because it takes away the beginner's deadly all-in weapon. It also forces more sophisticated post-flop play.

If pot-limit hold'em were the game played at the World Championships, you'd see less and less Cinderella stories at the final table.

8. The game is all luck.

People still believe this nonsense. This misconception comes from people who don't understand poker or haven't figured out how to win at it.

There are thousands of skilled professional poker players in the world, which distinguishes poker from other forms of casino gambling, like craps, keno, and Let it Ride. I assure you, there are no professional Let it Ride players.

9. You can't beat low limit games.

I've met several people who feel they can't win at low limit tables because too many players see the flop and then stick around until the river. While a game like this will certainly increase your stack fluctuation, and might make you feel like you're less in control, there isn't a more profitable game in the house.

If you're losing in lower limit games, playing higher limits is not the answer.

10. You need a poker face.

This one's probably the longest standing myth on the list. People commonly believe that you need a poker face to win. Well, watch me play on television and you'll see that I don't have a poker face at all. I'm generally joking around and making all kinds of goofy faces.

35.

Playing the Player

You'll often hear the expression, "playing the player," as it relates to poker. I want to share with you what it actually means, as well as give you some tips on how to do it.

Legendary poker champion Doyle Brunson once said about a no-limit game he played in, "I could beat that game without even looking at my cards." He wasn't being cocky or disrespectful towards the other players. Doyle was just supremely confident in his ability to play the players. He could read them so well that the cards became irrelevant.

Obviously, he couldn't win if his opponents knew that he wasn't looking at his hole cards, but if Doyle played his position properly, he felt like he could pull it off.

How, you ask, can you win at no-limit Texas hold'em without looking at your cards? It's not easy, but let me give you a few key points to consider.

Position

Position is power. When it comes to playing your opponents, being able to see their actions before you act is a huge advantage.

When they check, bet a little bit, or even overbet the pot. These actions will give you key information as to the strength of their hands.

With some players a check means that they don't have anything at all. Others might have a telltale sign of overbetting the pot when they're bluffing. If you are in tune with your opponents' tendencies, you can use your position to steal pots from them.

Reading Tells

This part isn't easy, especially if you aren't adept at reading body language. However, this skill can be learned.

Your brain really does process information like a computer. Just by being focused and paying attention, you'll pick up player information you don't even realize you're subconsciously acquiring. The next time you see an opponent betting his chips a certain way, your subconscious will send a message to the conscious part of the brain—something like "Suspicion alert! I've seen that somewhere before and it means he's bluffing!"

When you talk to a player like Jennifer Harman, in my opinion, the best female poker player in the world, about why she made a certain call, she'll say something like, "I don't know. I just felt he was bluffing."

Well the truth is, while Jennifer doesn't necessarily know why she made the call, it was no fluke. Her subconscious told her something was suspicious about the way her opponent bet his chips.

If you're able to read body language tells that reveal the strength of your opponent's hand, it will make beating him so much easier. Imagine knowing that when he bets with his left hand he's bluffing, and when he bets with his right hand, he has a really strong hand. How could you ever lose?

Scare Cards

Doyle Brunson is a master at combining position and reading tells to determine the strength of his opponent's hand. Yet there is one more piece to the puzzle. Doyle can get inside his opponent's head and figure out what he's holding, and just as importantly, what he's not holding. I'll explain.

If Doyle knows what type of hand a competitor is holding, he'll also be able to figure out what board cards will scare the opponent.

Let's say, for example, Doyle calls a tight, conservative player who raised from early position. Doyle won't even have to look at his hole cards. Instead, he'll combine position, tells and the board cards to outplay his opponent.

Okay, now the flop comes 8♥9♥7♠, and Doyle's opponent bets the whole pot. Based on previous hands against this player, Doyle believes that his opponent has to have a hand like A-A, K-K, or Q-Q. So, without ever looking at his cards, he makes the call.

Then the turn card comes 10♥. The opponent checks, and Doyle can now steal the pot by representing either the straight or the flush. His opponent can't call.

That's just one example of how it's done. Keep in mind, however, that in order to be able to consistently outmaneuver your opponents, you need to have position, pay attention to their body language, and also be able to use scary board cards to your advantage.

36.

Suited Connectors

"Texas Dolly" Doyle Brunson changed the way poker would be played forever when he wrote *Super System* so many years ago. In that legendary bible of poker, Doyle introduced some new poker concepts that, until then, only he and a few other professional players truly understood.

This specifically refers to one of those concepts: How and when to play suited connectors. Back in the days when Doyle was cleaning up with his aggressive style, most of the other players played close to the vest and waited for high card combinations like A-A, A-K, or K-Q.

Once Doyle understood that his opponents would never play so-called garbage hands like 6-7 suited, it became easier for him to read his rivals. He knew that little cards on the flop likely wouldn't help his opponents. He also knew that his opponents either started with a pair or that they likely had two high cards like Big Slick, A-K. With this information, Doyle cemented his reputation as one of the best who's ever played the game.

So then, why would you want to play a suited connector

hand like 7♣8♣ if you know that your opponents are starting with strong hands?

Well, because in no-limit hold'em, it's not what you start with that counts, it's what you end up with. If you're holding small suited connectors, and for a relatively small percentage of your stack you can stay in to see the flop, there are several benefits:

1. If you happen to get lucky with that 7♣8♣ and hit a flop like 4-5-6 or 8-7-3, you'll often trap an opponent with an overpair like A-A, K-K, or Q-Q.

2. It adds unpredictability to your game. Playing cards at every end of the deck will make it much more difficult for your adversaries to get a read on you.

3. Now here's the best part. You'll actually be able to bluff more! This may sound strange to you but think about it. If your opponents catch on to the fact that you play all sorts of *funny cards*, you'll be able to bluff them on the flop when you don't improve your hand.

For example, if you played a hand like Q-J suited, and the flop came 4-5-6, you could still win this pot. How? Well, your opponents may fear that you are playing the little cards again and flopped two pair or maybe even a straight. Even if they have Big Slick, there's a decent chance that they'll throw it in the muck making you the winner.

Doyle also discussed the concept of limping in with suited connectors by just calling the big blind to see the flop cheaply. Unfortunately, once the book came out, better players recognized that those limp-ins usually signified a suited connector, sometimes a small pair, or, in rare cases, a strong hand like A-A or K-K looking to set a trap.

So, my advice is to take your game one deceptive step

further. If you're holding suited connectors, throw out some small raises from time to time. This way, people won't know if you have A-A, A-Q, or 6♦8♦. Mixing up your play by throwing in the occasional raise with relatively weak suited connectors will go a long way toward making you a dangerous and tricky player. That's exactly the type of player that you want to be and that most people fear.

When deciding if it makes sense to play suited connectors, there are several things you should think about:

1. Your stack size.

If you are on a short stack, you won't get the implied odds you would with a big stack. On a short stack you need to avoid these hands and look for cards that are higher in rank.

2. The size of the bet.

You can't call raises with suited connectors if the size of the bet is too big a percentage of your stack. Ideally, you want to invest only a small percentage of your stack when trying to hit a home run.

3. If you don't hit the flop, well, abort mission!

Don't get stubborn. These are tricky hands to play, and if you don't improve with a good flop, you need to dump the hand and move on. You'll get other chances later.

When you see me playing poker on TV, you'll notice that I take my own advice. You'll often find me in there with some strange-looking hands, but, rest assured, there is method to my madness. Add some suited connectors to your repertoire from time to time, and you will see your overall results improve.

That is a guarantee.

37.

Heads-Up with Jerry Buss

At the first-ever National Heads-Up Poker Championship, my first round opponent was none other than Los Angeles Lakers owner, Dr. Jerry Buss. Jerry was one of just a handful of celebrity players in a tough field of 64 that also included the likes of actor James Woods, and poker professionals Johnny Chan and Doyle Brunson.

Drawing Jerry in the first round was supposed to make it easy for me, but he is no slouch at the table, having played countless hours of high stakes poker against some of the world's best.

If you caught that episode on television, you would have seen me make a miraculous prediction to finish off the match. Not only did I predict that precisely the 8 of diamonds would fall on the turn, but also that the last card would be the jack of diamonds, giving me a straight flush to beat Jerry's ace-high flush.

How did I do it?

I have absolutely no idea. The odds of calling two

consecutive cards are astronomical, and I'll predict this too—I'll never do it again the rest of my life.

As improbable as that was, it's not the hand I want to talk about.

There was a crucial hand earlier in the match where I had a chance to knock Jerry out of the tournament. Instead, I threw the hand away. It's a laydown I might not have made in most situations because of the standardized rules in tournament play.

All of the major tournaments in the United States share the following rule: You may not show your opponent your hand until the action is complete, or you will receive a penalty (usually 10 minutes on the sidelines while your chips are anted off).

However, the rule for the Heads-Up Championship allowed a player to show his opponent a hand any time he wished.

Why would anyone want to do that, you ask? Well, often you can pick up a tell on your opponent based on the way he reacts to seeing your hand. If you show him a better hand, for example, he may get nervous. Vice versa, if you show him a hand that he can beat, he may appear more relaxed.

So I found myself in an interesting situation against Jerry when he bet all of his remaining chips on the river, with a final board of Q-10-3-A-9. Jerry had first checked, then called on the flop, and when the ace hit on the turn, we both checked. On the river, the 9 gave me two pair, queens and nines, and Jerry bet about $8,000. If I called with my two pair and won, it would be all over. If I called and lost, I'd be letting Jerry right back into a match that I was dominating at the time.

So that's when I decided to take advantage of the "show your hand" rule and let Jerry take a look at my cards.

Jerry glanced over at my two pair and genuinely didn't look worried. In fact, his reaction was one of relief more than anything.

I started talking aloud as I often do while I play.

"Jerry, what do you want me to do here?" Without much hesitation, Jerry replied, "Well, I'd like you to call, actually."

I believed him. He even kind of smirked when he said it. There was so much evidence pointing toward Jerry having me beat. I couldn't ignore it. I folded the hand.

One of Jerry's biggest strengths in life, but biggest weaknesses at the poker table, is that he is an honest man. Jerry wouldn't have been able to tell me an outright lie like that without feeling guilty. He's too honest!

I went on to win the match a few rounds later with my straight flush.

That's when Jerry told me that he just had a pair of queens in the earlier hand—but, in fact, he didn't.

"So you bluffed me then, Jerry? Nice play," I said.

"No, I didn't bluff you. I had queens and tens," replied Buss.

As I said, Jerry is an honest man. He lied to me for a split second and then immediately felt guilty and had to reveal the truth. And least I think he did.

When I finally watched the broadcast at home, all of my suspicions were correct. Jerry had precisely queens and tens.

The lesson in this story is that poker is more than just about the cards you are dealt. It's about people, understanding human nature, and basically learning what makes them tick.

Unfortunately for Dr. Buss, I had him pegged as an honest guy and my read was dead on.

38.

Why the House Always Wins

Poker is very different from other casino games.

The first thing you have to realize is that the gaming giants don't keep building luxurious casinos because gamblers consistently win in Las Vegas. The house games are designed so that the casino always has an edge over the player.

So face it, you'll never have an edge in casino games like roulette, craps and Let it Ride. Even in pai gow, where the odds are as close to 50-50 as you're going to get, the house still maintains an edge.

Why? Well, every time you win you have to pay the house a 5 percent commission. That might not seem like much at the time, but those small edges are enough for Las Vegas to make billions off tourists with dreams of hitting it big.

So what makes poker any different?

The casino has no vested interest in who wins or loses. You aren't playing against the house. Instead, you're basically renting a seat from them.

Poker players should look at the house more like a landlord than as an adversary. Depending on the casino, your rent comes in one of two forms: either a rake, or what's called, a *collection*.

In a **raked game**, the house takes a percentage of the pot each hand. A typical rake in a $5/$10 limit hold'em game will be something like 5 percent, up to a $3 maximum. If the total size of the pot is $20, the house will rake $1. If the pot is $60 or more, the house will still take the maximum rake of $3.

In higher limit games, however, the house charges a **collection**. This means that every half hour they'll require a certain amount from each player. In a $10/$20 game, the collection might be something like $5 per player, per half hour.

There are some minor strategic adjustments you should make depending on whether or not the house is taking a rake or charging a collection. You see, in a collection game, it doesn't matter how many small pots you win, as you'll be paying the house a set amount every thirty minutes.

In a raked game, though, the more pots you win the more you are essentially paying for your seat. So speaking very generally, you should play slightly more conservatively in a raked game and more aggressively in a collection game.

Also, look to get involved in multiway pots with lots of value. If you're playing in a tight, raked game, many of the hands you play will be heads-up or three-handed, which isn't good for you.

Here's an extreme example: Imagine you are playing one on one against an opponent. If the house is taking a $3 rake per hand, it's very likely that neither you nor your opponent can possibly come out ahead. In an hour, they will be dealing approximately 60 hands. At $3 per rake, that would mean that collectively the two of you will be paying a $180 cover charge per hour!

Compare that to a collection, where the house might charge each player $10 per hour.

I think you can see which fee structure makes more sense.

Understand this too: If you're playing at a table with a

high rake, it's very important that you find a game where there is a lot of action with several callers before the flop. If it's a tight game, with mostly heads-up pots, it's probably a no-win proposition for all the players.

Also, in a high rake game, remember to play both more conservatively and more passively to encourage your opponents to stay in the hand. Conversely, in a collection game, even if the play is very tight, you can operate super fast and loose, since you won't be punished for winning more pots than the others.

If you have a choice, you should almost always go with a collection game. Sure, sometimes you'll have to pay for the hour—even though you didn't win a single hand—but in the long run, it's going to save you a ton of money.

39.

Bankroll Management

Making good decisions based on your current financial situation might just be the most important element you'll deal with when playing poker. You'll often be at the mercy of the cards, since there is undeniably an element of luck in poker. The deck will ultimately decide your fate.

For that reason, you should establish strict rules for yourself that define how much money you're willing to risk and what limits to play.

Let's say, for example, you have $1,000 that you've set aside as your poker bankroll. You'll need to know what games you can afford to play, budget-wise and skill-wise.

Here are two important questions you'll need to ask yourself.

1. Am I skilled enough to beat these players?

Generally speaking, the higher the limit, the more skilled the player. So, if you're new to poker, it makes sense to start at the bottom in the lowest limit game available.

2. How important is this $1,000 bankroll to me?

If it's your life savings and you can't afford to lose it, well, frankly, you shouldn't be playing poker with it. No matter how big your bankroll, lady luck can take it all away from you in a heartbeat. However, there are some things you can do to protect yourself from losing it all.

In most poker books, authors will tell you that you should have 300 big (blind) bets as an adequate bankroll. That's a pretty safe kitty. In fact, if you're a solid player who wins one big bet per hour, there's only a 3 percent chance of ruin if you stick to the appropriate limit.

If you have a $1,000 bankroll, the correct limits for you to play will be between $1/$2 and $2/$4. If you want to be on the safe side, a $1/$2 game affords you a bankroll of 500 big bets (1,000/2 = 500), while, if you're more of a risk taker, the $2/$4 game leaves you with only 250 big bets (1,000/4 = 250).

Now, if you feel like your skill level is good enough to win at the $1/$2 table, you might want to take a shot at a $2/$4 game. When I say take a shot, it's important to understand that I don't mean risking the entire $1,000.

Instead, you could invest $400 in a $2/$4 game. If you were to lose it, you'd still have the bankroll to go back down in limits with your remaining $600 and still have the required $300 big bets. The key to surviving is having the discipline to swallow your pride, take your lumps, and then move down in limits if things don't work out at a higher limit game.

By the way, lack of discipline isn't solely the domain of amateurs. In fact, some of the most talented poker players in the world are currently broke, and they'll habitually go broke, time and time again, due to poor bankroll management.

However, for every hard-luck story, there are the professionals who combine solid play and solid bankroll-management skills.

You'll find many of them at the biggest cash game in the world, at the Bellagio in Las Vegas.

And just in case you're pondering the idea of playing in that $4,000/$8,000 mixed game with the world's best, you'll need a bankroll of at least $2.4 million to give yourself a chance. You might be the best poker player in the world, but if you sit down in that game with *only* $500,000, you'll end up broke most of the time.

If you've learned anything thus far it should be that it's important to take your time, play it safe for the most part, and don't be in a rush to play higher and higher limits.

Living the life of a serious poker player can be stressful enough all by itself. The last thing you want to do is compound that by continually adding financial pressure to the mix.

40.

Poker Math and Conditional Probability

Figuring out how to do poker math doesn't require a PhD in mathematics. In fact, if you got past the 3rd grade, and know how to multiply and divide, you should be just fine.

One important aspect of poker math entails figuring out the probability of a card coming to improve your hand, and another, assessing the likelihood of your opponent holding a certain hand.

Let's say, for example, that you know for certain that a player will only raise with A-A, K-K, or Q-Q from early position. Now, suppose that player raises and you're looking down at pocket cowboys—a great K-K pair.

You'd try to figure out whether or not you have the best hand, and you'd conclude that the probability is 50-50. If your opponent has the other K-K, that's a wash, leaving just the Q-Q and A-A. The aces have you beat, you can tie the kings, and you can beat the queens at the moment.

Now suppose I tell you that the player from early position would raise with *any* two cards in that position. In this situation, the odds of your K-K being the best hand are closer to 99 percent. That's a simplistic view of conditional probability, of course, so let's look at a more complex example.

Suppose you are at the final table of a no-limit Texas hold'em tournament and are dealt A-A. The player to your right goes all-in with a massive overbet, and you decide to just call, hoping that another player might enter the pot.

Then, to your delight, the small blind, a top professional player, also calls. His bet tells you that he also has a strong starting hand. The flop comes 6-6-4. The pro player checks to you and you decide to get tricky by checking yourself.

Now the turn card comes with an ace, giving you a monster full house. The pro bets just a little bit, and once again, you decide to slowplay your hand by just calling. The river brings another 6, for a final board of 6-6-4-A-6.

The pro now checks to you, and it's your turn to act. The dilemma you face is this: You know that he won't call you unless he has the ace in his hand, but he will check-raise you all of your remaining chips if he has the last 6 for the four of a kind nuts.

Since there is just one 6 and one ace remaining in the deck, that leaves the odds at 50-50, right?

In a tournament setting, where survival is so important, it might just be wise to check this hand in case the pro was setting a trap for you with four of a kind.

According to probability, it's just as likely that he has an ace in his hand as he does a six. Not so fast. Let's take a closer look at the hand and take into account the overall situation. For the pro player to call an all-in raise in that position, isn't it much more likely that he has an ace versus a 6?

Let's take it a step further.

If the pro player did call a raise with a 6 in his hand, what would be his most likely side card? Well, he couldn't have started with 6-6 because there are three sixes on the board, which leaves just A-6. Not only that, you'd then have to wonder whether or not he would check four of a kind on the river, rather than bet out himself.

That is a stretch and a half. When you factor in conditional probabilities, in this particular situation, it would be extremely unlikely that the pro has the last 6. In fact, that 50-50 probability starts looking more like 99-1 in your favor. I'd even go as far as to say that if this was truly a pro player, the odds of him holding a 6 in this situation would be nil.

One of the biggest mistakes players make when trying to calculate odds and figure out probability is that they neglect to consider conditional probability.

The more you know about your opponent's tendencies, the more accurately you can calculate the probability of what he is holding. Always remember, it's not solely about what your opponent's cards are. You must consider how he plays them, too.

41.

Pot Odds

When you watch poker on TV, you hear the term *pot odds* thrown around all the time. What in the world does it really mean? Well, hopefully, after reading this you'll not only know what pot odds are, but you'll also understand how to quickly calculate pot odds and apply them to your game.

A simple generic definition of the term **pot odds** would be the odds the pot is laying you in comparison to the bet you are facing.

For example, if there is $500 in the pot and your opponent has bet $100, your pot odds would be 6 to 1. Why? Well, because there is already $500 in the pot and your opponent has bet an additional $100 for a total of $600. Since you need to call $100 to stay in the pot, your odds are 6 to 1.

Simple enough, right?

So how exactly do you apply this basic knowledge to a poker hand? Here's how to figure out your pot odds, compare them to your actual odds, and then use this information to make an informed decision as to whether or not you should continue playing the hand.

Step 1: Figuring the pot odds

This is the easy part. You count what's already in the pot and add it to the amount of the bet you are facing. You then compare that sum to the amount your opponent has bet. So again, if there was, for example, $200 in the pot and your opponent bets $20, your pot odds would be 11 to 1 ($220/$20).

Okay, so now that you know what your pot odds are, it's time to figure out if you are getting the right price to continue playing the hand.

Step 2: Figuring your actual odds

This can be a little more difficult depending on the situation. You can find a table of actual odds in almost any poker book on the market. Another option is to pick up some simulation software that will calculate the odds for you. But since you obviously won't have access to a book or software right there on the spot, here's how to figure out your actual odds while seated there at the table.

The first thing you need to do is count your **outs**, meaning the number of remaining cards that will improve your hand. Then, compare that number to the total number of unseen cards still in the deck. Here's an example.

Let's say the board reads K♣7♠6♦2♥, and in your hand you hold 8♥9♥. With just one card to come on the river, you have eight outs: the four remaining fives and the four remaining tens to make your straight.

There are 52 cards in the deck, and since you already know what your two cards are, as well as the four community cards on board, that leaves 46 unseen, unknown cards. Of those 46 cards, eight will give you a winning straight, while 38 will miss. So the actual odds of making your straight then are 4.75 to 1 (38/8= 4.75 to 1).

Since you know the pot odds are 11 to 1 and your actual

odds of improving your hand are 4.75 to 1, you can see that you're getting a great return for the investment and should call. If, however, there were only $20 in the pot and your opponent bet $20 then the pot odds would be only 2 to 1, and you wouldn't be making a good investment at all by calling the bet. In this example, even though you have eight outs, the correct play would be to fold the hand.

The goal in poker is relatively straightforward and simple. It's not about how many pots you win. The goal is to make good investment decisions, as in any other business venture. By understanding pot odds, you can make educated decisions as to whether calling or folding would be good long-term investments.

As is true in the stock market, if you make good decisions in the short-term, you'll make a decent profit in the long run.

42.

Soft Playing is Cheating: Play Hard or Don't Play

What I'm about to say may surprise you. You might be a cheater and not even know it.

If you are in a poker game for money and are taking it easy on one of your buddies, you are cheating yourself, your friend, and every other player in the game. I realize that's a bold statement, but it's absolutely true.

In the poker world, we have a term for this type of play. It's called soft playing. When two friends, spouses, relatives or flat-out cheaters don't bet against each other, they're soft playing.

Soft playing destroys the integrity of the game of poker and it's wrong, dead wrong.

I realize that many players have no idea that this behavior is so unethical. More often than not, soft playing (not to be confused with *slowplaying*) is done innocently with no harm intended. Perhaps a gentleman doesn't want to take a lady's last $20. Or, one player doesn't want to raise his friend because his friend is losing too much money.

Well, if you are so concerned with your buddy losing money, or if you're trying to get a date by not betting against a beautiful woman, try taking them both out to dinner after the game. The poker table is no place for compassion and kindness. I'm sort of kidding, but I think you get the idea.

The unintended by-product of soft playing a friend is how it affects the action for the rest of the players at the table. For example, let's say that you and a pal both make the final table of a no-limit Texas hold 'em tournament that pays the top five finishers. There are six players remaining and you and your buddy are still hanging in. Remember, the next player out gets nothing. Everyone at the table wants to see someone get knocked out so that they can finish in the money.

How do you think the other players at the table would feel if you are soft playing your friend?

By not playing hard against him, you are absolutely cheating the other players at the table. That may not have been your intention, but ignorance of the rule won't get you off the hook when you get caught. Soft playing in a tournament can result in severe penalties, including disqualification to both you and your friend.

Poker is not a team sport. It's every man for himself. It's perfectly okay to root for your buddies and hope they do well, but when it's time to play the game, you have to give it your all.

All by yourself, that is.

I've seen far too many pacts between players end up in shambles. I remember a husband and wife who used to play together. They agreed that they wouldn't bet or raise against each other. When the wife lost a pot to another player because the husband didn't raise with a hand he was supposed to, she chewed him out.

"But Honey, I thought we said we wouldn't raise each other?"

"Ah, forget that, you turkey, give me your best game or you're sleeping on the couch!"

Arrangements like that always end up ugly. In order for

you to do well, and for fairness to prevail, you have to play hard against everyone at the table. That includes Grandma, Grandpa, Aunt Betty, and little Timmy.

I mean, really, if you can't check-raise your mother, what kind of player are you anyway?

Soft playing is, more often than not, totally innocent. But you need to be aware that there are snakes out there, and it's important that you spot them before they team up against you.

If you're playing online and you smell something fishy, e-mail customer support and have them investigate. At reputable poker sites, a representative will look into your claim by reviewing the hands in question, as well as the betting history of the suspected cheaters. If suspicious betting behavior is detected, the crooks will be banned from the site and you will likely receive a refund for the money you lost due to player collusion.

If you see something strange in a live game, notify the floor man immediately and ask him to investigate.

43.

Setting Up a Home Poker Tournament

Before you decide to enter the big time arena of million-dollar poker tournaments, you might want to practice your craft at home with friends first. All you really need to set up a tournament are some cards, poker chips, a table, and, oh yeah, breathing bodies.

Of course if you want to be a good host, you might want to provide some munchies and beverages, too.

Depending on what your guests are comfortable with, the first thing you'll have to agree on is the buy-in for the tournament. You can play for as little as pride or as much as $100 per person. Not surprisingly, when there's actual money being wagered the excitement level is usually higher. Playing socially for $20 a head should satisfy everyone's competitive spirit and provide a decent prize to shoot for.

Once you've decided on the entry cost, the next step will be drawing for seats. If you have ten players, pull out one ace through ten and have each guest randomly pick a card and take the appropriate seat.

Then decide on the amount of chips to start with, the blind

structure, how long each round will last, and finally, the payout. For maximum fun, here's what I suggest.

1. Starting chips.

Start every player with $10,000 in chips, and remember, you don't have to actually play for $10,000 to start with that many chips. Give each player the following: one $5,000 denomination value chip, three $1,000 chips, two $500 chips, and ten $100 chips.

If you don't have enough chips to make this happen, play around with other chip combinations. Having four different chip colors will help move the game along quickly.

2. Blind structure.

You want to make sure that you start the blinds small enough so that everybody gets a chance to play for a while. On that note, I would suggest using the following blind structure:

Round 1:	$100 small blind, $200 big blind
Round 2:	$200 small blind, $400 big blind
Round 3:	$400 small blind, $800 big blind
Round 4:	$800 small blind, $1,600 big blind
Round 5:	$1,000 small blind, $2,000 big blind
Round 6:	$1,500 small blind, $3,000 big blind
Round 7:	$2,000 small blind, $4,000 big blind
Round 8:	$3,000 small blind, $6,000 big blind

Depending on how much time you have and how skillful you want the tournament to be, you can add or take away rounds accordingly. The more rounds there are, the more expertise is needed to win.

3. Length of rounds.

One method is to choose a time limit—ten or fifteen minute rounds should do the trick. Another option is to have the blinds escalate after every lap around the table. For example, if you start the dealer button in Seat One, every time the button returns to that seat, increase the blinds. If Seat One is eliminated, then raise blinds when the button returns to Seat Two.

I like this method best because it speeds things up later in the tournament so that eliminated players won't have to wait around too long without playing.

I've played in many house games before, and we never have just one tournament. Everyone will be anxious to get back in the action, so the faster you raise the blinds, the less time your guests will have to wait around and raid your fridge!

4. Spoils to the winners.

You'll need to consider how to divide up the money, if you play for money at all. Typically, you'll have three options: winner takes all, pay 1st and 2nd place, or pay the top three finishers.

If you have ten players putting up $20 each, you'll have a $200 prize pool. The best payout structure to ensure that your guests don't get hurt too bad financially is to pay the top three places. The 1st place finisher gets 50 percent of the prize pool or $100. The 2nd place winner earns 30 percent or $60. The 3rd place player takes home 20 percent or $40.

The best way to decide on the payout structure is to provide three options and have the players vote on which one they like best.

Remember, when hosting a tournament poker party, your main concern should be in making sure that everyone is happy and having a great time.

Well, that and trying to win all the money.

44.

Heads-Up Poker

The National Heads-Up Poker Championship pits 64 of the best players in the world against each other, head to head, in a bracket format. I absolutely love this tournament because I believe that heads-up poker is the most skill-oriented form of the game.

In some ways, heads-up poker is less about playing the actual cards you are dealt and more about playing your opponent. The goal is to find your challenger's weaknesses and then exploit them. All the while, you're trying to mask your own strategy so that he doesn't figure you out.

When it comes to heads-up play, there is one absolute: You really need to get in there and fight. Conservative play isn't effective at all in a heads-up match. In a full ring game, with 9 or 10 players, sure, you can sit back and wait for premium cards if you like. If you are playing heads-up, however, your starting hand requirements must be lowered considerably. In fact, most limit hold'em experts agree that when battling heads-up you should play well over 80 percent of the hands dealt to you. Contrast that to playing approximately 20 percent of the hands dealt to you in a full ring game. Nearly the same holds true in no-limit hold'em, but the percentage may not be quite as high.

The key reason that you need to get more involved when playing heads-up is that you're forced to ante up every single hand. The player with the dealer button must post the small blind while the other player puts up the big blind.

By the way, this is the only situation in hold'em where the button is ever forced to act first. After the flop, play resumes as normal with the button acting last on every subsequent street.

The best way to improve your heads-up game is to actually get your feet wet and play. You can do that on the Internet at numerous free sites, or if you're feeling adventurous you can play for real money. Of course, you can also just practice with friends.

Improving your heads-up play will have a positive effect on your overall skill level, even at a full table. The decisions you are forced to make in heads-up are often so much more complex than those you would ponder at a full table. Practicing these tough decisions makes the routine decisions just that—routine. Imagine shooting hoops on a very small and tight rim. If you got adept doing that, then making baskets on a regular-sized rim would seem very easy to you.

When playing heads-up, your main focus must be on what your opponent is doing. Is she playing weak or strong? Does she bluff too much or is she always betting only the strongest hands? The more questions you can successfully answer, the better profile you'll have on your opponent.

Once a profile is established, it's then your job to devise a strategy that will best exploit your opponent's weakness. For example, if she folds too often on the flop, then you should bluff more on the flop. Or, if she folds too much before the flop, you should raise more often prior to the flop. Conversely, if your opponent calls too often, you should bluff her less and bet your mediocre hands for more value.

There is one other key thing you need to focus on—yourself.

Do not allow yourself to fall into predictable patterns that your opponent will be able to exploit. You don't want to play every hand the same way. Use all of the tools in your arsenal: the check-raise, the slowplay, coming over the top, the bluff raise on the turn, and even the smooth call on the flop. This is commonly known as **mixing it up**. Mixing it up keeps your opponent guessing, and that's exactly where you want him to be.

Here's one final thought on the game. You must avoid coming into a heads-up match with a predetermined strategy. Until you have an idea as to how your opponent might play, that strategy of yours may be the wrong one. It's important to be able to adapt quickly to what the other player is throwing at you.

45.

What to Look for in Heads-Up Poker

There are some significant differences between playing heads-up poker and more common poker games where six to nine players compete at a table. The type of hands you should play, and the way you should play them, are very different from a standard game.

Here are a few things to look for whenever you watch heads-up play.

Who is the aggressor?

In heads-up play, the player who employs a more aggressive style will generally come out on top. The reason is rather simple. Because it's so difficult to hit a flop, true heads-up poker skills are shown when both players have absolutely nothing after the first three community cards are dealt. The player who consistently wins this trench warfare is the one who will usually win the overall battle.

Who is the caller?

When you continue to put yourself in situations where

you're facing an opponent's bet, it becomes increasingly more difficult to make correct decisions. For that reason, you want to be the bettor, not the caller.

Checking and calling can be a viable strategy to trap a player. However, if you're always in a situation where you're guessing the power of an opponent's hand, guess what, you'll end up guessing wrong too often.

Trapping an opponent is an art form. It can be done many different ways using a myriad of poker tools. One notable method is to *slowplay* a hand. Slowplaying can be dangerous, though, because you might give your opponent a chance to catch a lucky card on the river to beat you.

The key to being a successful trapper is to not get caught in the trap yourself! If your trap fails, you have to be willing to abort the mission and change strategies quickly.

Let's say, for example, in a heads-up match, you just call before the flop holding a pair of kings. Now the flop comes A♠7♥4♣. Sure, you started with a very powerful hand, but this flop is dangerous and puts your cowboys in peril. If your opponent holds an ace, only two cards left in the deck can save you.

While you tried to set a trap, it didn't spring as you hoped. Proceed with caution. Don't let yourself lose a big pot after that flop.

Another important element you should look for during heads-up play are the escalating blinds. As the blinds continue to increase, the quality of hands that players go all-in with will diminish.

In the first round of play, for example, if two players go all-in before the flop, you'll likely see a confrontation like K-K versus Q-Q, or even A-A facing K-K. However, after about the fifth level, the blinds become so large that both players will gamble more loosely in defense of their blinds. By that point, it's common to see all-in pots where one player may hold a hand as weak as A-3 and the opponent calls all-in with K-10.

In my opinion, heads-up poker is the wave of the future. More and more people are playing it today than ever before. You can even qualify for the National Heads-Up Poker Championship by playing online. That's exactly what Josh Lochner did. He beat out 30,000 other hopefuls to win his spot in the 2006 Championship's exclusive 64-player field.

46.

Playing Short-Handed

There hasn't been much discussion in poker books dealing with the topic of playing in a *short-handed* game, that is, playing against a small number of opponents.

Most Texas hold'em games are played with nine, ten, or even eleven players seated at the table. In a game like this, you can afford to sit tight, and wait for premium hands before entering a pot. Since you only have to pay a blind twice per round, the pressure to play lots of hands just isn't there.

When you're playing short-handed, however, you are forced to play more hands since each one you throw away will actually cost you more money. Let me explain.

Let's say you're sitting in a ten-handed hold'em game with $5/$10 blinds. One round circling the table would cost you $15 total if you didn't play a hand. That's an average of $1.50 per hand ($15/10 hands), which doesn't seem too bad, but look what happens when you cut the number of players from ten to five.

Now, a lap around the table costs the same $15, but you'd only get to see five hands. That means, on average, it will cost you $3 for every hand you fold. If you take that a step further, in a three-handed game, you'd be paying $15 to see just three hands. That's $5 per hand!

The ante and blind structure dictates how loosely you should be playing. If, for example, there were no blinds or antes at all, it would be silly to play any hand in hold'em other than pocket aces. However, since you do have to pay a penalty for waiting for the best cards, playing only A-A would cause your chip stack to get anted off, round by round.

Okay, that should help explain why it's important to play more hands in a short-handed game. It's also important to understand what hands you should add to your repertoire, and how you should play them.

In short-handed games, hands that do well *hot and cold*, meaning that they could win without improvement, go up in value, while speculative hands, like 7-6 suited, go down in value.

It's very different at a ten-handed table.

A hand like 7-6 suited does very well when there are five or six players seeing the flop. Something like K-7 offsuit doesn't fare as well. Conversely, the K-7 does much better in short-handed situations than does the 7-6 suited.

In short-handed play, it's also more important to maintain an aggressive style than it would be in a full ring game.

In a full game, if a player raises from early position and you, in middle position, hold a pair of fours, there is no need to even get involved with the hand. You can safely fold since you have nothing invested.

In a five-handed game, however, this would be an opportunity to get aggressive and reraise before the flop. Yes, I understand that it's a small pair, but a 4-4 is still the favorite to win, even against the Big Slick, A-K, heads-up.

As a rule, short-handed play is more of a battle for the antes, while full ring game play is more about waiting on premium cards in good situations. There isn't as much pressure to play, because the blinds don't come around as fast.

That's why so many players seem afraid of playing a short-handed game. It's high-stress, high-energy poker that forces you to make complex decisions with much weaker hands.

Frankly, short-handed games are where stronger players thrive while weaker opponents simply get pushed around.

47.

World Series of Poker

Without a doubt, the World Series of Poker (WSOP) is the richest event in sports, and it grows by leaps and bounds each year. Since 1970, when there were just a handful of players starting this great tradition, the number of entrants slowly increased—until recently.

Today, we're seeing an explosion that's changing the event forever and has caused poker to reach heights no one could have ever imagined. When Chris Moneymaker, a complete unknown, won it all in 2003, there were an astounding 839 players, up over 300 players from 2002.

ESPN's coverage of the Moneymaker phenomena opened the floodgates, and in 2004 we saw 2,576 players pony up $10,000 each trying to be the next Moneymaker—literally and figuratively. That year, Greg "Fossilman" Raymer became the third straight nonprofessional player to win the most coveted title in poker.

It was virtually a given that the 2005 no-limit Main Event would once again break the record for number of entrants. Online poker sites held small satellite tournaments where wannabes could qualify for the most prestigious event in poker for as little as $9.

The final count in 2005 was 5,619 players for a whopping $56.6 million prize pool, with the winner earning $7.5 million. Only about 300 of those players were pros. So, once again, an amateur was expected to win it all. Why? It's a simple numbers game.

In years past, when the tournament attracted 200 to 300 players, well over half of the entrants were professional poker players. While the number of pros hasn't risen dramatically, the number of amateurs willing to put up ten grand of their own money has skyrocketed.

Which begs the question: Will a top professional ever win the WSOP main event again? I think so, but because of the sheer number of entrants, it's certainly not going to be a favorite to happen.

Don't get me wrong, the pros are still the favorites. If you could bet on the 300 pros versus 300 amateurs, you'd be a large favorite. That's not how it works, of course, but I think you see my point.

In 2005, you would have been hard-pressed to call anyone at the final table a loser. When Mike "The Mouth" Matusow was eliminated in ninth place he represented the last remaining professional. Luckily, for Mike, that ninth place finish netted a cool one million bucks. Not bad for a week's work!

Of the eight remaining players, not one had ever won a world championship bracelet at the WSOP. All eight were relative unknowns. Joseph Hachem of Melbourne, Australia ultimately beat out Steven Dannenmann of Severn, Maryland, and instantly became a poker celebrity.

A week prior, no one in the poker world had ever heard of these two men. Now they sure have. They're known to millions around the world thanks to ESPN.

There's one colossal thing that separates poker from other sports you'll watch on TV. You'll never bask in the glory of Wimbledon. You'll never experience the thrill of hitting a three-pointer at the buzzer to win Game 7 of the NBA Finals. You'll never have the chance to chip in for birdie on 18 to steal the Masters crown from Tiger Woods.

But you might be able to bust Phil Hellmuth, or bluff out Phil Ivey, or even take down a huge pot from that blonde-haired, earring-wearing guy with the goatee, and actually win the Holy Grail of poker.

For poker purists, however, the World Series of Poker will never be the same.

Look at the WSOP Wall of Champions—Johnny Chan, Doyle Brunson, Johnny Moss, Stu Ungar, all legends in the poker community. It gives you goose bumps. Many wonder if those days are gone forever. The nostalgic club of gamblers is making way for a more corporate-run lottery: poker for the masses.

The pros shouldn't be complaining too much, though, as they're getting a hefty pay raise. Some use their sudden fame to sell products, while others are just cashing in on tournaments with much larger prize pools.

As recent as 2001, 9th place in the main event paid $91,910. In 2006, Jamie Gold earned $12,500,000 for his first place finish.

Complaining? Who's complaining!

48.

Exploiting Your Table Image

Understanding how people perceive you at the poker table is often as important as knowing which cards to play. In fact, the most important adjustment I was forced to make, in order to beat the world's best players, was to become aware of how my play was affecting my table image.

Here's an extremely simple example to illustrate my point. Let's say that in a fifteen-minute span you've been caught bluffing four times. Well, if your opponents are even slightly perceptive, they'll notice that tendency. Further bluffing is going to be much less effective. That fact will either help you or hurt you depending on how well you adjust to your perceived table image.

In one sense, your bluffing spree will likely cause your opponents to call you with much weaker hands. They're hoping that you're still bluffing. When you do catch a very strong hand, you won't have to do anything tricky to ensure getting full value for the hand.

On the other side of the coin, you have to be aware that

your bluffs will be called more often, so you'd be wise to tighten up your play and wait for better starting cards.

There are pros and cons to being pegged as a mad bluffer. You'll no longer be able to steal pots that you might otherwise have been able to take down with a timely bet. But at the same time, you'll get full value for your strong nonbluffing hands. As you can see, although your table image is established, you can make adjustments to exploit that image and use it to your advantage.

Here's another example: You've been playing for five hours and haven't been dealt many good cards. It's been one fold after another, making it look like you're playing very conservatively. The few hands you've played were very powerful ones.

Well, this tight, conservative table image also has its pros and cons. Your opponents notice that you play like the Rock of Gibraltar, and that when you bet, you always have a monster hand. Use that table image to your advantage and steal some huge pots! Since everyone has you pegged as Mr. Tight Guy who only plays the nuts, your bets will get significant respect.

You can profit from this conservative table image as well. Yes, you'll lose a little value when you have a strong hand, but you'll more than make up for it when you have a weak hand and bluff at a huge pot.

Other behaviors will also have an impact on your table image.

Let's say that you've been on a killer rush and are winning every pot in sight. Your opponents may begin to fear you, thinking, "Man, this guy is just too lucky." On top of that, your positive frame of mind will disturb players who are losing so many pots to you. This is an excellent table image to cultivate and will cause your frustrated opponents to make more errors.

Conversely, if you're running very unlucky—losing every pot on the river—your opponents will likely attempt to take advantage of you. They'll presume that you're on tilt since you've been losing so much. This gives them even more confidence.

In this situation, don't let them see you sweat, and don't complain or cry. Your opponents should never know that your cold streak is affecting you. When you're getting beat up at the tables, you simply need to take your lumps and walk away.

Of course, when the cards are coming and your table image is working, that's the time to exploit it. That's when you want everyone to know how you're feeling. Say something like, "Man, I'm just hitting every hand. The cards keep coming and coming!"

Reinforce your image of being "too lucky" and you'll maintain a psychological edge over your opponents.

49.

Dealing with Bad Beats

I'm probably asked this poker question more than any other. How do you deal with bad beats?

It's a relevant question, especially considering how important it is to be able to handle those painful stings of bad luck that you'll inevitably encounter.

There are definitely some do's and don'ts when it comes to dealing with bad beats. Let's first look at a few of the don'ts.

1. Don't tell bad beat stories.

Do you want a sure-fire way of guaranteeing that nobody will talk to you? Just tell them how unlucky you've been and how they wouldn't believe the hand you just lost with.

Look, they really don't care. Bad beats happen to everyone.

I mean, seriously, have you ever looked forward to someone telling you a hard-luck story? Keep your bad beats to yourself.

2. Don't go on tilt.

What often happens to players when their luck runs bad

is that they start playing poorly. They go on tilt. They chase hands they normally wouldn't or try something new because, hey, playing good cards just isn't working.

Reacting in this manner will wreck your game. You don't have to try something new. You need to focus more keenly on playing well and sticking to your game plan despite the bad run of cards.

3. Don't let your opponents see you sweat.

If they know you've been running bad, their confidence against you will soar. They will surely look for the opportunity to attack. Like sharks circling their prey, once they see you're wounded, they'll move in for the kill.

You must keep your composure at the poker table and not let bad beats affect your play. Staying calm and focused will go a long way towards making a quick recovery.

Keep this in mind, too: When players ask how your cards have been running, it's a trick. Answer shrewdly by saying, "Pretty good, actually. I've been on a nice streak lately." You might know that the cards have turned to ice, but your opponents don't need to know it. Remember, deception is fundamental to the game of poker.

And now for some of the do's to help you get out of the bad beat blues.

1. Take some time off.

This is the absolute best way to reenergize your batteries when the cards start spitting in your face. You need a clear head so that you can focus on making good decisions.

When you start wondering how your pocket pair of aces is going to lose the next hand, you are in desperate need for some downtime!

2. Play smaller limit games.

It's often difficult for players to move from their regular limit games to a smaller limit game, but that's exactly what I recommend that you do.

Swallow your pride and regain your confidence by playing against (and beating) weaker players in smaller limit games.

3. Stay positive.

If you believe you're an unlucky player, you'll become one. It's a self-fulfilling prophecy, and it's true in any facet of your life.

Focus on making correct decisions at the poker table and not on the outcome. That's how the best players approach the game of poker.

Yes, I realize that maintaining composure and staying positive is easier said than done. I've been there before, too. All poker players have been there before. When you start thinking you are the unluckiest player in the world, I can assure you that it's a tie. You and about a million other players can make that claim.

For some poker players, it's often "If only I were as lucky as that scrawny little goateed guy with two earrings. I could beat him, but he's too lucky."

You'd better believe that I'm lucky, and not just in poker. I'm lucky in life because I was raised by two wonderful parents, I have my health, and I live in a free country.

If you focus on all of the good things you have going on in your life, all of a sudden, a bad run of cards just doesn't seem so important now, does it?

50.

Final Thoughts

I hope you enjoyed reading this book as much as I enjoying writing it. You probably noticed a couple of recurring themes throughout each of these short chapters. Each defines my approach to winning, and hopefully, will add to your enjoyment and success in the game.

If you want to become a better player, a winning player, first and foremost, you'll need to learn the fundamentals of the game. Read a variety of poker books, watch poker on television, and of course, gather as much playing experience as you can—in cardrooms and home games, on the Internet, and in tournament play.

Also, make sure to think outside the box. It's not enough to simply memorize how to play certain hands, it's important to understand why the hand should be played that way. Poker is a beautiful game with so many variables, you can't play it with a defined set of rules as you would in blackjack. Don't be afraid to experiment with different strategies. Even if they fail, you will have learned something.

One final thing: Play the game with style and grace. There

is just no good reason to be a jerk at the poker table. By being a nice guy, I think you'll find that you'll do better in both poker and life. And, always be respectful of your competition—while you try to take all their money!

For more money-making titles, visit us online!
www.cardozapub.com

FROM CARDOZA'S EXCITING LIBRARY
ADD THESE TO YOUR COLLECTION - ORDER NOW!

SUPER SYSTEM by Doyle Brunson. Jam-packed with advanced strategies, theories, tactics and moneymaking techniques, this classic work,widely considered to be the most important poker book ever written! Chapters are written by six superstars: Mike Caro, Chip Reese, Dave Sklansky, Joey Hawthorne, Bobby Baldwin, and Doyle—two world champions and four master theorists and players. Essential strategies, advanced play, and no-nonsense winning advice on making money at 7-card stud (razz, high-low split, cards speak, declare), lowball, draw poker, and hold'em (limit and nolimit). A must-read—every serious poker player must own this book. 628 pages, $29.95.

SUPER SYSTEM 2 by Doyle Brunson. The most anticipated poker book ever, SS2 expands upon the original with more games and professional secrets from the best players in the world. Superstar contributors include Daniel Negreanu, winner of multiple WSOP gold bracelets and 2004 Player of the Year; Lyle Berman, 3-time WSOP gold bracelet winner and founder of the World Poker Tour; Bobby Baldwin, 1978 World Champion; Johnny Chan, 2-time World Champion and 10-time WSOP bracelet winner; Mike Caro, poker's greatest researcher, theorist, and instructor; Jennifer Harman, the world's top female player; Todd Brunson, winner of more than 20 tournaments; and Crandell Addington, no-limit legend. 672 pgs, $34.95.

CARO'S BOOK OF POKER TELLS by Mike Caro. One of the 10 greatest poker books, this must-have classic should be in every player's library. If you're serious about winning, you'll realize that most of the profit comes from being able to read your opponents. This book reveals the the secrets of interpreting *tells*—physical reactions that reveal information about a player's cards—such as shrugs, sighs, shaky hands, eye contact, and more. Learn when opponents are bluffing, when they aren't and why—based solely on their mannerisms. Over 170 photos of poker players in action and play-by-play examples show the actual tells. These powerful eye-opening ideas can give you the decisive edge at the table. 320 pages, $24.95.

CARO'S GUIDE TO DOYLE BRUNSON'S SUPER SYSTEM by Mike Caro. Working with World Champion Doyle Brunson, the legendary Mike Caro has created a fresh look to the "Bible" of all poker books, adding new and personal insights that help you understand the original work. Caro breaks 36 concepts into the following categories: analysis, commentary, concept, mission, play-by-play, psychology, statistics, story, or strategy. Lots of illustrations and winning concepts give even more value to this great work. 86 pages, 8 1/2 x 11, $19.95.

CARO'S FUNDAMENTAL SECRETS OF WINNING POKER by Mike Caro. Learn the essential strategies, concepts, and plays that comprise the very foundation of winning poker play. Learn to win more from weak players, equalize stronger players, bluff a bluffer, win big pots, where to sit against weak players, and the six factors of strategic table image. Includes selected tips on hold'em, 7-card stud, draw, lowball, tournaments, more. 160 pages, $12.95.

7-CARD STUD: The Complete Course in Winning at Medium & Lower Limits by Roy West. Learn the latest strategies for winning at $1-$4 spread-limit up to $10-$20 fixed-limit games. Covers starting hands, third to seventh street strategy for playing most hands, overcards, selective aggressiveness, reading hands, secrets of the pros, psychology, and more in a 42 lesson informal format. Includes bonus chapter on 7-stud tournament strategy by World Champion Tom McEvoy. 224 pages, paperback, $19.95.

MILLION DOLLAR HOLD'EM: Limit Cash Games by Johnny Chan & Mark Karowe. Learn how to win money at limit hold'em, poker's most popular cash game. You'll get a rare opportunity to get into the mind of the man who has won 10 World Series titles—tied for the most with Doyle Brunson—as the authors pick out illustrative hands and show how they think their way through the bets and the bluffs. No book so thoroughly details the thought process of how a hand should be played, how it could have been played, and the best way to consistently win. 368 pages, paperback, $29.95.

GREAT CARDOZA POKER BOOKS
ADD THESE TO YOUR LIBRARY - ORDER NOW!

CRASH COURSE IN BEATING TEXAS HOLD'EM *by Avery Cardoza.* Perfect for beginning and somewhat experienced players who want to jump right into the action and play cash games, local tournaments, online poker, and the big televised tournaments where millions of dollars can be made. Both limit and no-limit hold'em games are covered, along with the essential strategies needed to play profitably on the pre-flop, flop, turn, and river. The good news is that you don't need to memorize hands or be burdened by math to be a winner—just play by the no-nonsense basic principles outlined in this book. There's a lot of money to be made and Cardoza shows you how to go and get it. 208 pages, $14.95

WINNER'S GUIDE TO TEXAS HOLD'EM POKER *by Ken Warren.* You'll learn how to play every hand from every position with every type of flop. Learn the 14 categories of starting hands, the 10 most common hold'em tells, how to evaluate a game for profit, the value of deception, the art of bluffing, eight secrets to winning, starting hand categories, position, and more! Includes detailed analysis of the top 40 hands and the most complete chapter on hold'em odds in print. Over 400,000 copies sold! 224 pages, $16.95.

HOW TO PLAY WINNING POKER *by Avery Cardoza.* New and completely updated, this classic has sold more than 250,000 copies. Includes major new coverage on playing and winning tournaments, online poker, limit and no-limit hold'em, Omaha games, seven-card stud, and draw poker (including triple draw). Includes 21 essential winning concepts of poker, 15 concepts of bluffing, how to use psychology and body language to get an extra edge, plus information on playing online poker. 256 pages, $14.95.

KEN WARREN TEACHES TEXAS HOLD'EM *by Ken Warren.* This is a step-by-step comprehensive manual for making money at hold'em poker. 42 powerful chapters teach you one lesson at a time. Great practical advice and concepts with examples from actual games and how to apply them to your own play. Lessons include: starting cards, playing position, raising, check-raising, tells, game/seat selection, dominated hands, odds, and much more. This book is already a huge fan favorite and best-seller! 416 pages, $26.95.

OMAHA HIGH-LOW: Play to Win with the Odds *by Bill Boston.* Selecting the right hands to play is the most important decision you'll make in Omaha high-low. More than any other poker game, Omaha is driven by hand value. This is the *only* book that shows you the chances that every one of the 5,278 Omaha high-low hands has of winning the high end of the pot, the low end of it, and how often it is expected to scoop all the chips. You get all the vital tools needed to make critical preflop decisions based on the results of more than 500 million computerized hand simulations. You'll learn the 100 most profitable Omaha high-low starting cards, trap hands to avoid, 49 worst hands, 30 ace-less hands that can be played for profit, and the three bandit cards you must know to avoid unnecessarily losing hands. 248 pages, $19.95.

POKER TALK: Learn How to Talk Poker Like a Pro *by Avery Cardoza.* This fascinating and fabulous collection of colorful poker words, phrases, and poker-speak features more than 2,000 definitions. No longer is it enough to know how to walk the walk in poker, you need to know how to talk the talk! Learn what it means to go all in on a rainbow flop with pocket rockets and get it cracked by cowboys, put a bad beat on a calling station, and go over the top of a producer fishing for a gutshot to win a big dime. You'll soon have those railbirds wondering what *you* are talking about. 304 pages, $9.95.

HOW TO WIN AT OMAHA HIGH-LOW POKER *by Mike Cappelletti.* Clearly written strategies and powerful advice shows the essential winning strategies for beating Omaha high-low poker! This money-making guide includes more than 60 hard-hitting sections on Omaha. Players learn the rules of play, best starting hands, strategies for the flop, turn, and river, how to read the board for both high and low, dangerous draws, and how to beat low-limit tournaments. Includes odds charts, glossary and low-limit tips. 304 pgs, $19.95.

THE CHAMPIONSHIP SERIES
POWERFUL BOOKS YOU <u>MUST</u> HAVE

CHAMPIONSHIP HOLD'EM TOURNAMENT HANDS *by T. J. Cloutier & Tom McEvoy.* An absolute must for hold'em tournament players. Two legends show you how to become a winning tournament player at both limit and no-limit hold'em games. Get inside their heads as they think their way through the correct strategy at 57 limit and no-limit starting hands. Cloutier and McEvoy show you how to use skill and intuition to play strategic hands for maximum profit in real tournament scenarios and how 45 key hands were played by champions in turnaround situations at the WSOP. Gain tremendous insights into how tournament poker is played at the highest levels. 368 pages, $29.95.

CHAMPIONSHIP WIN YOUR WAY INTO BIG MONEY HOLD'EM TOURNAMENTS *by Brad Dougherty & Tom McEvoy.* Every year satellite players win their way into the $10,000 WSOP buy-in event and emerge as millionaires or champions. You can too! Learn from two world champions, the specific, proven strategies for winning almost any satellite. Covers the 10 ways to win a seat at the WSOP, how to win limit hold'em and no-limit hold'em satellites, one-table satellites, online satellites, and the final table of super satellites. Includes a special chapter on no-limit hold'em satellites! 320 pages, $29.95.

CHAMPIONSHIP TOURNAMENT POKER *by Tom McEvoy.* Enthusiastically endorsed by more than five world champions, this is a *must* for every player's library. McEvoy lets you in on the secrets he has used to win millions of dollars in tournaments and the insights he has learned competing against the best players in the world. Packed solid with winning strategies for 11 games with extensive discussions of 7-card stud, limit hold'em, pot and no-limit hold'em, Omaha high-low, re-buy, half-and-half tournaments, satellites, and includes strategies for each stage of tournaments. 416 pages, $29.95.

HOW TO WIN NO-LIMIT HOLD'EM TOURNAMENTS *by Tom McEvoy & Don Vines.* Learn the basic concepts of tournament strategy and how to win big by playing small buy-in events, graduate to medium and big buy-in tournaments, adjust for short fields, huge fields, and slow and fast-action events. Plus how to win online no-limit tournaments. You'll also learn how to manage a tournament bankroll and get tips on table demeanor for televised tournaments. See actual hands played by finalists at WSOP and WPT championship tables with card pictures, analysis and useful lessons from the play. 376 pages, $29.95.

POKER TOURNAMENT TIPS FROM THE PROS *by Shane Smith.* Essential advice from poker theorists, authors, and tournament winners on the best strategies for winning the big prizes at low-limit rebuy tournaments. Learn the best strategies for each of the four stages of play—opening, middle, late and final—how to avoid 26 potential traps, advice on rebuys, aggressive play, clock-watching, inside moves, top 20 tips for winning tournaments, and more. Advice from McEvoy, Caro, Malmuth, Ciaffone, others. 160 pages, $19.95.

NO-LIMIT TEXAS HOLD'EM: The New Player's Guide to Winning Poker's Biggest Game *by Brad Daugherty & Tom McEvoy.* For experienced limit players who want to play no-limit or rookies who have never played before, two world champions give readers a crash course in how to join the elite ranks of million-dollar, no-limit hold'em tournament winners and cash game players. You'll learn the four essential winning skills: how to evaluate the strength of a hand, how to determine the amount to bet, how to understand opponents' play, and how to bluff and when to do it. 74 game scenarios and two unique betting charts for tournament play and sections on essential principles and strategies, show you how to get to the winners circle. Special section on beating online tournaments. 288 pages, $24.95.

CARDOZA POKER BOOKS
POWERFUL INFORMATION YOU MUST HAVE

CHAMPIONSHIP NO-LIMIT & POT-LIMIT HOLD'EM by *T. J. Cloutier & Tom McEvoy.* This is the bible of winning pot-limit and no-limit hold'em tournaments. You'll get all the answers here—no holds barred—to your most important questions: How do you get inside your opponents' heads and learn how to beat them at their own game? How can you tell how much to bet, raise, and reraise in no-limit hold'em? When can you bluff? How do you set up your opponents in pot-limit hold'em so that you can win a monster pot? What are the best strategies for winning no-limit and pot-limit tournaments, satellites, and supersatellites? Rock-solid and inspired advice you can bank on from two of the most recognizable figures in poker. 304 pages, $29.95.

CHAMPIONSHIP HOLD'EM by *T. J. Cloutier & Tom McEvoy.* Hard-hitting hold'em the way it's played *today* in both limit cash games and tournaments. Get killer advice on how to win more money in rammin'-jammin' games, kill-pot, jackpot, shorthanded, and full table cash games. You'll learn the thinking process before the flop, and on the flop, turn, and river with specific suggestions for what to do when good or bad things happen. Plus 20 illustrated hands with play-by-play analyses, specific advice for rocks in tight games, weaklings in loose games, experts in solid games, how hand values change in jackpot games, when you should fold, check, raise, reraise, check-raise, slowplay, and bluff. Also tournament strategies for small buy-in, big buy-in, rebuy, add-on, satellite and big-field major tournaments. Wow! If you want to win at limit hold'em, you need this book! 392 pages, $29.95.

CHAMPIONSHIP OMAHA (Omaha High-Low, Pot-limit Omaha, Limit High Omaha) by *Tom McEvoy & T.J. Cloutier.* Clearly-written strategies and powerful advice from Cloutier and McEvoy who have won four World Series of Poker Omaha titles. Powerful advice shows you how to win at low-limit and high-stakes games, how to play against loose and tight opponents, and the differing strategies for rebuy and freezeout tournaments. Learn the best starting hands, when slowplaying a big hand is dangerous, what danglers are and why winners don't play them, why pot-limit Omaha is the only poker game where you sometimes fold the nuts on the flop and are correct in doing so, and, overall, how you can win a lot of money at Omaha! 296 pages, illustrations, $29.95.

CHAMPIONSHIP TABLE (at the World Series of Poker) by *Dana Smith, Ralph Wheeler, & Tom McEvoy. Championship Table* celebrates three decades of poker greats who have competed to win poker's most coveted title. This book gives you the names and photographs of all the players who made the final table, pictures the last hand the champion played against the runner-up, how they played their cards, how much they won, plus fascinating interviews and conversations with the champions. This fascinating and invaluable resource book includes tons of vintage photographs. 208 pages, $19.95.

HOW TO WIN THE CHAMPIONSHIP: Hold'em Strategies for the Final Table, by *T.J. Cloutier.* If you're hungry to win a championship, this is the book that will pave the way to success! T.J. Cloutier, the greatest tournament poker player ever—he has won 59 major tournament titles and appeared at 39 final tables at the WSOP, both more than any other player in the history of poker—shows how to get to the final table where the big money is made and then how to win it all. You'll learn how to build up enough chips to make it through the early and middle rounds and then how to employ T.J.'s own strategies to outmaneuver opponents at the final table and win championships. T.J. shows you how to adjust your play depending upon stack sizes, antes and blinds, table position, opponents' styles, and chip counts. You'll also learn the specific strategies needed for full tables and for six-handed, three-handed, and heads-up play. 288 pages, $29.95.